COUNTDOWN TO PARTY TIME!

Children's Party Ideas
guides you every step of the way . . .

- PICKING A PLACE FOR THE PARTY
- MAKING THE GUEST LIST
- SENDING THE INVITATIONS
- PLANNING GAMES, REFRESHMENTS, AND FAVORS
- DECORATING FOR THE SPECIAL DAY
- CHOOSING A THEME
- ORGANIZING AND BUDGETING
  and more!

Children's parties are always fun. Now planning them can be fun, too—and easier than ever before, with . . .

CHILDREN'S PARTY IDEAS

CHILDREN'S PARTY IDEAS

Margaret Dunne

BERKLEY BOOKS, NEW YORK

CHILDREN'S PARTY IDEAS

A Berkley Book / published by arrangement with
Boldface Publishing

PRINTING HISTORY
Berkley edition / August 1994

ISBN: 0-425-14344-9

BERKLEY®
Berkley Books are published by The Berkley Publishing Group,
200 Madison Avenue, New York, New York 10016.
BERKLEY and the "B" design
are trademarks belonging to Berkley Publishing Corporation.

PRINTED IN THE UNITED STATES OF AMERICA

10 9 8 7 6 5 4 3 2

Contents

CHILDREN'S PARTY IDEAS

Planning a Party

A child's birthday party can be as much fun for the parent as for the child. Planning and putting on a great party is really quite simple; it's just a matter of organizing a few key elements: invitations, decorations, gifts, refreshments (cake and ice cream!), party favors, and some activities to keep the guests amused and entertained.

All of these elements are discussed at least generally in the following pages, and some of the more essential or difficult elements are discussed in greater detail.

There's one piece of advice to always remember: don't get stressed out—this is, after all, a party!

Keep in mind that this is a party for your child, not a major community project or career move. Your child won't notice if some small detail goes wrong, and will probably have more fun if you are also having fun than if you are uptight and worrying about details.

By all means include your child in the planning. This gives the child a chance to participate in planning a major social event, a skill which will be very useful in the future.

Planning the party together minimizes the risk of disappointments on the special day. This is especially important for younger children who tend to get over-excited when they are the center of attention and are being surprised. If the child helps to plan the party, he or she knows what to expect and will be ready to react appropriately.

With older children, planning the party together makes sure you don't embarrass the child in front of peers by doing something that is "out." And, unless you are part of the group, you certainly don't have much more than a foggy clue as to what is "in" or "out" at any given moment.

Involving children in the planning also gives them more to look forward to, as well as providing a great chance for the family to work together on a project.

General Planning

Begin planning one to three weeks prior to the party, depending on the size and complexity of your proposed event. A first decision is whether to do-it-yourself at home, or plan a party away from home—at a fast-food place or other recreation facility. This decision must take into account a number of factors—not the least of which is what your child prefers. At the same time, be sure your child (and you!) are not just caving in to peer pressure. A chance to show up the neighbors is not a good reason for planning an extravagant birthday party outing.

Also remember, when planning the scope of the party, to inventory your physical, emotional, and financial resources. Don't tackle more than you can realistically handle.

A Theme?

Deciding on a theme for the party makes the planning process much easier. A theme gives you a general direction and some boundaries. The theme helps you come up with ideas for everything from the invitations to decorations, favors, and food.

But don't worry about coming up with an elaborate theme if you don't have the time, energy, or creativity. You already have a built-in theme—The Birthday Party! For very young children, this is the only theme you really need or should have. One- and two-year olds are too young to appreciate or participate in any theme beyond the party itself.

For older children, more specialized themes might be built around their special interests, hobbies, some current fad or fancy, or the season.

If your child is fascinated by sports, try a sports theme. If your child builds model airplanes, try an airplane theme. If some current movie or cartoon characters have captured her fancy, build a party around that theme.

Seasonal parties might include ice-skating in the winter, a fall pumpkin-patch visit, a spring garden party or a summer beach party.

See Chapter 6 for dozens of theme party ideas and appropriate suggestions for food, activities, and decorations for each of them.

Age Group Planning

Keep all the guests at a party fairly close together in age. With younger children, even those of the same age can have greatly different levels of development.

Keep in mind that much of the fun for kids is in planning and anticipating the party; therefore, stay away from surprise parties until the kids are preteens or teenagers. Even for a child of that age, a surprise party can be risky unless you have a clear idea of who his or her best friends are, and get them involved in the planning.

For very young children (ages one and two) you'll generally want to have at least one parent accompany each child. Babies and toddlers really have no idea what the party is all about, and won't remember it, so there's no need to do very much.

For two-year-olds, you can just invite a few favorite adults to celebrate with cake, or one or two other two-year-olds with their parents.

It's at about ages three and four that the children will start to have an idea what the party is all about, but kids at this age are easily excited. Keep the party short, tightly structured, and plan quiet activities that won't overstimulate them.

Kids start to demonstrate interest in things such as movies, television shows, or dinosaurs at about five. This is a good age at which to start considering a theme party.

Sleep-over parties, same-sex parties, and parties away from home will be considered at about age seven or eight.

Budgeting

If you are on a limited budget, you can still have an enjoyable and memorable birthday party.

With younger children especially, there is no need to do much more than making a nice cake and having a few activities planned. Younger children are easily entertained. And remember, the party is for the children, not for their parents. Don't get into the trap of thinking you need a party to impress all the parents. If the birthday child and the guests have a good time, the party is a success by any measure.

You can cut down on expenses by not serving a meal at the party. Schedule the party for mid-morning or mid-afternoon, and specify on the invitation that the party is for cake only.

If you or your child feel a party away from home is the way to go, you can still do it on a budget. Look for unusual, inexpensive alternatives to the usual commercial party places. And, if there is a per-person charge, keep the number of guests to a minimum.

You can generally save money by doing and making more yourself. Be resourceful. See what you have around the house that can be used to make invitations, decorations, and party favors. The typical house is full of interesting and valuable resources. See Chapter 2 for some ideas on doing these items yourself.

Do-it-yourself also applies to food, entertainment, and activities. You can save money by preparing the party food, making and decorating your own cake, and providing the entertainment, activities, and costumes. Again, there are some tips in the following pages to get you started in these areas.

When you need something for the party, don't immediately think of running to the mall; think first of free or inexpensive sources. Need a book or videotape? Try the library first. Need a costume? Try grandma's attic. Need some props to decorate the party room? Try a thrift shop or second-hand store, or even your own basement or garage. Not only will you save money, you'll be eliminating some clutter!

Choosing a Date

When choosing a party date, try to schedule the party for the child's actual birthday if possible, although this isn't critical. It is more important to have the party when all the most important people can attend. This includes both parents if appropriate. Not only is it important for the child to have both parents on hand, but it is good to have the extra help available.

If you aren't able to schedule the party for the actual birthday, have a small family observance on that day so your child doesn't feel neglected.

Second in importance to having key family members available is having the birthday child's best friends. The party won't be a success without them. Check with parents of best friends to make sure they are available before setting the date.

Keep preschool and kindergarten schedules in mind, too, and plan the party day and time accordingly.

Entertainment

If you are considering having an entertainer at your child's party, make sure the act is age appropriate. Keep in mind that clowns are scary to some young kids, and magicians too abstract.

Keep an act short for young kids, about twenty minutes, up to a maximum of forty-five to sixty minutes for older kids.

If you are hiring someone to impersonate a popular figure, be sure they know their character completely. Santa, for example, had better know all the reindeer names.

Have the entertainment at the start, when kids are alert, and in their best mood. Prepare the kids so they aren't scared by a large character doing strange things. Tell them what to expect.

When choosing an entertainer, make sure he or she is accustomed to working with kids in the age group you are hosting, get references, and brief the performer on any special circumstances of which to be aware.

Get detailed information on what the performance involves. Some performers provide small favors for each guest, which will eliminate that expense for you and help offset the cost of the entertainment.

If budget is a major concern, see if you can find a good amateur performer at a local high school, college, club, or youth group. When working with amateurs, it is even more important to get some references and work closely with them in planning the act.

Home or Away?

Traditionally, children's birthday parties have been celebrated at home, and many parents and children still value that tradition. But children, and to some extent their parents, are seeing the fun and ease of having the party away from home.

For one thing, you get to come home after the party to a clean house. On the other hand, consider the age group of the party (kids under age five might prove a hard-to-manage group) and consider that the novelty of a trip to a local fast-food outlet may have worn off if three or four kids in the group have already had parties there.

There are a number of options in choosing a party place away from home. Some national restaurant chains offer special party packages, so you don't need to go to the same one every time. Also, many family-oriented community attractions have gotten into the profitable business of hosting parties. Some possible locations:

- A local children's museum
- A theme park
- A family amusement center
- A zoo
- A public library
- A children's theater (or a movie theater)
- A community center
- A skating rink (ice or roller)
- A miniature golf course
- A bowling alley

If you do decide to have a party away from home, examine the full array of possibilities available in your community.

If you want a new idea, see if your community has a "parents" newspaper, which generally has a number of ads geared to party ideas. Or browse through the Yellow Pages under "Amusement Places."

At Home Parties

For parties at home, keep the party to a limited area. This minimizes the mess, eases the clean-up afterwards, and makes it easier to monitor the action.

For parties during nice weather, you will want to consider having the party outdoors. (In fact, certain theme parties almost demand being held outdoors.) But if you do plan an outdoor party, make sure you have an alternative for moving the party indoors if the weather turns bad.

Use decorations and other methods to clearly mark off the party area, and be firm about keeping the party in this space. Set up a spot beforehand for guests to put their coats, as well as a collection place for gifts.

Don't worry too much about cleaning the house; it's just going to need another cleaning after the party. The kids certainly won't notice if the house is spotless; just pick up enough so any adults attending aren't scandalized. Once the party gets under way there will be enough confusion and enough mess that nobody will ever be able to tell what state the house was in before the party started.

Safety Check

If you are having the party at home, chances are you've already child-proofed your house for the age group involved. If you are going to have the party at the home of a grandparent, relative, or friend without children in the age group involved, give the house a good safety check.

The safety check is of particular importance for outdoor

parties. If you have a pool, be sure that it is secured. Check for sharp points or splinters on any fences or play equipment the children will be near. Check for poisonous plants, and be sure not to apply any toxic chemicals to the lawn for several days prior to the party.

Check the lawn carefully for any hidden objects, such as lawn sprinklers or roots on which a child might trip or be injured. Give the lawn a good raking to pick up any hidden objects, such as broken glass.

Indoors or outdoors, if you have pets, decide what to do about them during the party. Even the most docile animal might get testy after an hour with a house full of five-year-olds.

Be sure to have enough adult or teenage helpers on hand to monitor activities and to keep an eye on all the guests at all times.

Finally, be sure to have some basic first-aid supplies on hand, just in case.

The Detailed Party Plan

Make a list of everything that will need to be done immediately before, during, and after the party. Assign yourself, your partner, or one of your helpers to each task. Be realistic. This tells you right away whether you will need more help. It also reminds you of those little essentials you might have forgotten: when you assign someone to videotape or take pictures, you remember to get tape, film, or batteries before the party instead of during the party!

Make up the list when you first start to plan the party, one to three weeks in advance. Review it once a week, and go over it carefully on the two days immediately before the party.

Here is a simple checklist to get you started. Make your own to include particular needs:

Item	Who Is Responsible?
General plan, theme	
Guest list	
Invitations	
Invitations mailed	
Party location, area chosen	
House cleaning	
Birthday cake	
"Child-proofing" as necessary	
Decorating	
Pre-party activities	
Menu planning & shopping	
Snack service, supplies	
Meal service, supplies	
Cake service, supplies	
Gift opening	
Favors	

Item	Who Is Responsible?
Prizes	
Entertainment	
Party games, activities	
Game & activity supplies	
Photo/video (film, tapes & batteries)	
Clean-up (supplies, trash bags)	

Parties Away From Home

For parties planned away from home, consider most of the above items, but also add:

Select location	
Reservations	
Transportation	
Menu	

When you are looking at places to hold an away-from-home party, keep notes for each place you contact. This will help in making your final decision, in discussing a final choice with your partner and child, and in finalizing plans when you call back to make the actual reservations and arrangements.

Make a copy of the following Party Location Information form. Record the information, and any other you feel is appropriate, for each place you contact:

Party Location Information

Name of establishment: _____

Person I spoke with: _____

Address: _____

Minimum or maximum guests? ____ Min. ____ Max.

Guest age limits: _____

Adult chaperone requirements: _____

Party time limit? _____

Deposit required? _____

Reservation deadline: _____

Outside food permitted: _____

Service fee: _____

Per guest cost: _____

Services included: _____

Menu available: _____

Hours available: _____

Dates available: _____

Special attractions: _____

**Special considerations
  for birthday child:** _____

Any problems, concerns? _____

**Reservation made
  (date and name)** _____

Notes:

Finding Help

Plan to have one adult (or responsible teenager) for every
five guests up to five years old, and one supervisor for
every eight guests for older kids.

The best source of help in running a party is your own
family. Naturally, your partner should be involved; the
birthday child's siblings if there are any, and if they are
mature enough; and grandparents are good bets if they
enjoy this sort of activity.

Make an arrangement with one of the other children's
parents: ask them to help monitor your party, and you will
help with theirs.

If friends and family aren't available, consider hiring
baby-sitters or high school kids who can double as part of
the entertainment (as clowns, or appearing in other theme
costumes).

Setting the Time

Set a firm time for the party to end, and let the parents of all the guests know the time. Generally, one or two hours is plenty long enough for younger kids up to about age ten. That is probably all you can tolerate, and the kids will have a better impression if they leave while they're having fun, rather than when they're bored, tired, and cranky.

Along those same lines, try to avoid evening parties for younger kids—they will be starting out tired and cranky.

Allow extra time for trips away from home, and for parties which include serving a meal.

Plan the party for a time when both parents can attend, even if this means scheduling for suppertime or on a weekend. This will allow both parents to share in the effort, and will make the birthday child feel even more special.

Make sure the guests' parents know exactly what time the party will end, and that the guests know, too. Older children who are not being picked up by a parent might need a gentle reminder that the party is over.

The Guest List and Invitations

The rule of thumb for the number of guests is one for each year of the child's age, plus or minus one. This number can be increased somewhat for older children.

If you are planning a long party (such as a slumber party) you might want to cut the recommended number of guests in half.

If you feel you can't limit yourself to a small number of guests, take a good look at the amount of space you have available and the amount of help you can recruit to keep an eye on all of the guests.

Invitations can be homemade, and can fit in with the theme of your party. Older children can help in making, addressing and mailing the invitations.

Always mail the invitations, rather than letting your child hand them out in school. This helps make sure the guests' parents know of the plan, and it helps to avoid hurt feelings when not everyone in your child's class is invited to the party.

Pre-Party Activities

Have activities planned that guests can join in on as soon as they arrive. This keeps them active and occupied until all have arrived, and the main party activities can begin. One easy activity for younger children is to have a large roll of paper and plenty of crayons or markers. Let the kids start on a mural which fits into the party theme.

Favors

You don't need to spend a lot of money on party favors: you might have the kids make their own as one of your party activities. This entertains the guests, and gives them something special to take home—something more special than an inexpensive trinket.

Browse through a craft shop or art supply store for ideas; maybe buy some inexpensive hats, T-shirts, or socks and have the kids decorate them with some of the new paints made especially for that purpose.

Or have them make something related to the theme of the party. Small boxes can be converted into treasure chests for a pirate party, for example.

See page 27 for some more favorite favor ideas.

Games

Plan plenty of games and activities to keep everyone occupied for the entire length of the party—and possibly beyond. You certainly don't want to have a dead half-hour until the parents arrive to pick up the guests.

Plan more activities than you think you will need. If something is falling flat, or just not working, move on to something else.

To keep all the party-goers in good moods, try to choose games which stress fun and cooperation rather than competition. Nobody likes to be a "loser," especially at a party in front of friends.

Entertainment

If you want to have more than do-it-yourself entertainment, you can save money and probably get a more enthusiastic performer by finding a talented amateur. Check with a community theater or local high school theater department, someone will know of an enthusiastic magician, ventriloquist, clown, or other entertainer suitable for your needs.

Ask for references from other parents who have had entertainers at parties for their children. If you can't find anyone, look for ads in a local "parents" newspaper, if your community has one, or in the Yellow Pages under "Entertainers."

Photo/Video Preparations

At least one day before the party, be sure you have plenty of fresh film or videotape. Be sure you have fully charged or fresh batteries.

Good advice for any one-of-a-kind event is to be sure you are comfortable with your equipment before the big day. If you have a new camera or video equipment, or if you just haven't used it in a few months, take some time to go over all the controls and operation. If you haven't used your camera in a long time, shoot a short roll of film and have it processed before the party. Shoot a few minutes of videotape using all the controls you expect to use at the party, and view it on your VCR.

If you are comfortable with your equipment, you can relax a little and enjoy the festivities even as you record the memories.

The Party Agenda

Plan the sequence of events for the party. A typical party goes something like this:

1. Greet guests, have some activity to keep them busy until all arrive.
2. Games, activities, entertainment.
3. Refreshments.
4. Open gifts, hand out favors.
5. Wind down activities.
6. Thank-yous and goodbyes.

Finally . . .

When all the plans have been made, do one final thing: imagine yourself giving the actual party. Imagine the guests arriving, getting them settled in the party area, opening gifts, playing the games and activities, serving the food, winding the party down, and getting the guests safely home.

This mental exercise should let you identify any problem areas, such as not having enough help to answer the door for late arrivals and monitoring the activities of the earliest arrivals.

During the Party

Don't forget to switch your mindset—your child is the guest of honor. Treat him or her as a guest while you and your helpers run the party and clean up afterward. Let your child keep the special party glow for as long as possible.

Photos or Video

If you followed the advice above and are fully prepared for the party, you can relax a little and enjoy yourself as you shoot the pictures or video.

Prepare the area you will be shooting in by opening all the shades or curtains, or turning on as many lights as possible. The more light you have the better the quality of your images.

Remember that you are trying to tell a story with your images, so imagine yourself as a photojournalist. You've probably noticed that news photographers are always running around at events they cover. What they're trying to do is to get enough of three different types of images to allow them to visually tell the story. They always want:

- "Long shots." A long shot is an overview, for instance a shot of the entire room or area where the party is being held. You can see the decorations, the guests, and get a flavor for the event and the action.
- "Medium shots." After you show the area, you should get some shots showing more detail of what's happening. Examples of medium shots would be cutting the cake, or several children involved in a party game.
- "Close ups." Of course, you'll also want plenty of close-ups of the guest of honor tasting the birthday cake, opening a gift, or just generally mugging for the camera. At least one close-up of each guest is also a good idea.

You don't see too many "extreme close ups" in the news, but they are more appropriate here—a full-frame shot of the party invitation, the inscription on the top of the cake, or some of the gifts will nicely round out your story.

When you are videotaping, try to remain more in the

journalist role than the Hollywood director role. Just record and describe the action, don't direct it. For example, which of these two narrations seems more informative and natural, and less intrusive:

"Here's Becky's friend Lynn enjoying her cake."

or

"Hey, Kate, look over here and wave at the camera!"

Some other tips:

- Get down. Kids are short and you are tall. If you shoot all your pictures from the standing position, you'll see a lot of tops of heads and craning necks. Sit on the floor or kneel down.
- Don't overdo the videotaping. If you shoot too many slides or pictures, you can easily edit them and just look at the most interesting ones. If you shoot three hours of videotape, you'll spend a lot of time being bored or using the fast-forward button. Just videotape the highlights, keeping the total tape time between thirty and sixty minutes.
- Stay steady. Use a tripod if you have trouble holding the video camera steady. And don't do a lot of fast zooms and camera movements.
- Don't put the camera away when the party is officially over. Get some shots of the birthday child saying goodbye to guests, enjoying a gift in private, or sharing a moment with parents.

Favors

Provide a small bag, basket, decorated box, or other container that each guest can use to carry home party favors, treats, and other items if necessary. Plan to have some extra favors on hand to avoid hurt feelings if one child's favor is broken by another guest or the birthday child, is eaten by the family dog, or simply lost in the course of the party.

Games

Make the games noncompetitive, or arrange it so that each child "wins" one of the games. This is especially important if there are prizes awarded. Plan the games so they become quieter as the party progresses, helping to get the children ready for the party to end.

Gifts

Some parents prefer not to have the child open gifts during the party, since everyone then wants to play with them. Also, with older children, there may be a subtle competition as to who brought the "best" gift.

If your child will open gifts during the party, structure it as a quiet activity. Have the birthday child sit and open one gift at a time, show it to everyone, and thank the giver.

If you do have the child open gifts during the party, as most parents do, have the birthday child give out party favors at this time, so that all the guests feel that they're also getting a present. This is especially important with younger children.

After the Party

Have some activities planned to let the kids calm down toward the end, and make sure you have enough to keep them busy if their parents are a little late in arriving to pick them up. See Chapter 9 for more discussion of winding the party down.

Invitations/
Decorations/
Favors

Next to the cake, the most important elements of a party are invitations, decorations, and favors. All of these items create an atmosphere that says "party," and that puts everyone in the party mood.

We all know the importance of making a good first impression, and that's just what a party invitation should do. It should shout "FUN" and put the invited guest in a party mood right away.

Decorations need to get guests into the party mood as soon as they get in the door.

And favors give each guest a little bit of party fun to take home, to keep as a memory of a great time.

All of these items can be made at home, or purchased. The choice depends on your budget, your available time, and your talent.

Having the birthday child help out in planning and creating the invitations, decorations, and favors can be an enjoyable family activity, and it helps to extend the special birthday feeling for the child.

21

Invitations

Invitations, as noted above, should immediately set a mood of fun, as well as set the theme, in the case of a theme party. At a minimum, invitations should include the following information:

Guest of Honor: Include the birthday child's name; the guest's parents may not know who it is. Also make it clear that it's a birthday party.

Date: Give the date and day of the week to eliminate any confusion: Saturday, August 22.

Time: Give the starting and ending time: Party begins at 1 p.m. and ends at 3 p.m.

Place: Give the exact address and include instructions if any of the guests or their parents are unfamiliar with the location.

Food: Indicate what type of food will be served (cake, snack, or meal) so the parents know how to plan meals.

Party Details: Is it a surprise party, a theme party, or a costume party? Should the child bring anything special, dress for indoors or out, or wear old clothes?

RSVP/Parent's Name and Phone Number: You should request a response by a certain date. This lets you know if all the birthday guests can make it, or at least whether there will be enough to insure a successful party.

Asking for an RSVP, or calling each guest's parent to remind them of the party, is a good idea for some more detailed planning. You can find out if the child has any food allergies or other problems which require preparation, you can give gift ideas if needed, and you can confirm any transportation needs.

Even if you don't request a response, you should include your name and telephone number so parents can contact

you if they have any questions, or if something comes up
at the last minute, or during the party, and they need to get
in touch with you.

Invitation Options

There are dozens of preprinted invitations available for
purchase at any grocery store, drug store, or card shop.
These are fine for any party, and may even be available
to fit in with many theme parties.

Purchasing a ready-made invitation may cost more than
making your own, or it may cost less. If cost is of concern
to you, figure out what it will cost to make invitations
which are appropriate, and compare the two choices.

Store-bought invitations will certainly eliminate the time
spent designing and making your own, which can be an
important factor.

The advantage of making your own invitations is that
they can be personalized to a much greater extent, can fit in
exactly with any theme party, and they can be much more
fun both to send and to receive.

Making Your Own Invitations

In making your own invitations, there is really no limit
to what materials you can use.

If the invitations are to be mailed, keep in mind that they
need to fit in an envelope or package, and that anything
larger or heavier than a standard envelope will require
additional postage.

On the other hand, if you make your invitation in the
form of a postcard, it will require less postage than a
standard envelope.

If you want to go all out and hand-deliver your invitations, there is really no limit to what you can do.

Materials to Make Mailed Invitations:

- Colored foil
- Confetti
- Construction paper
- Gift wrap
- Glitter
- Gummed stars
- Maps
- Photographs
- Postcards
- Poster board
- Ribbons
- Rubber stamps
- Stickers
- Tape

Browse through a craft store, stationery store, or art supply store to get many more ideas for invitation materials.

Ideas for Hand-Delivered Invitations:

- Bag of popcorn with invitation written on it
- Balloon with invitation attached
- Basket with treats and invitation in it
- Cupcake with invitation attached

High Tech Invitations

New home and office technology has opened up a number of new options for making very impressive and original invitations. Using a home computer, it is possible to create and print very imaginative invitations, and even personalize them for each guest.

If you already have a home computer, you probably have or know about a simple, inexpensive program which allows you to create fun party invitations, banners, and other similar items.

If you don't have a home computer, ask some friends who have them. If you have a computer but don't have a "print shop" or simple drawing program, check with a local computer store. These types of programs (*Print Shop* from Broderbund Software is an example) are generally available for about $40.

Many "quick" print and copy shops now have computers available for rent by the hour, allowing you to create special invitations; or, a member of your family might have free access to a school or office computer.

The copy machine can be enlisted in the process, as well: create one master invitation, then make a copy for each guest. You can buy colored paper (with matching envelopes) to put in a copier at your office, or have the invitations copied onto color paper at a copy shop.

Many larger copy shops now have color copiers, so you can make your master invitations using colored paper, stickers, markers, and even color photographs. Find out if color copies are available, and what they cost in your area, before counting on this option. They generally cost a dollar or more per copy.

These invitations can either be "generic" or part of a theme. Specific suggestions for invitations, decorations, and favors tied to a number of themes can be found in Chapter 6.

Decorations

Decorations can be generic—balloons, streamers, confetti and the like—or they can be specific to a party theme.

Look through Chapter 6 for some specific theme-related decoration ideas. In general, as long as you make the party area look different than it does normally, and as long as it puts everyone in the party spirit, that's all you need to worry about.

Here are some all-purpose decorating ideas:

- Pull out all your child's stuffed animals and place them around the party room.
- Find a number of inexpensive posters that fit into the

party theme. There is special tape that lets you hang posters without damaging the wall, or try rubber cement to hang lighter posters on painted walls—it will rub off afterwards.

• Make some mobiles using wire coat hangers and fishing line. Hang paper cutouts or small toys to fit the party theme. Install the mobile over the party table, or in the middle of the room.

• Make large bouquets out of balloons and crepe paper.

• Make your own murals or posters, or have posterboards or large rolls of paper on hand with plenty of colored markers for the guests to make their own decorations as they arrive.

Favors

Most kids aren't terribly picky about what they get as party favors. As long as they get a treat to take home with them, they're generally happy.

Party favors can be as simple as a decorated paper bag filled with candy treats and perhaps a small trinket or two. Just be sure that each child gets essentially the same favor, and that you have extras in case some get lost or broken in the excitement of the party.

If you can't find a good source of inexpensive favors in your community, try a mail order source. A good one is the Oriental Trading Company, Inc. Call for a catalog at 1-800-228-2269 or write to P.O. Box 3047, Omaha, NE 68103.

Favorite Favors

- activity books
- cards, card games
- clay
- coloring books
- crayons or colored markers
- hats
- marbles
- pocket games
- posters
- puzzles
- sticker books
- stickers
- story books
- T-shirts

Games and Activities

There are a number of things to keep in mind when planning games or other activities for a party. The games should be something the children like to do, and something they can do. Most importantly for a birthday party, a game should be something the guest of honor likes to do and is fairly good at. It is best to play games that involve all of the children all of the time. If they have to take turns, or if losers are eliminated as the game progresses, those not involved quickly become bored, if not unruly. If you have a large group of children, you may need to have one or more assistants, and divide the children up into smaller groups.

Try to avoid highly competitive games, particularly those where there is only one winner. Play games that allow everyone to win something. Team games help eliminate direct competition, and provide more fun and a better sense of participation for those children who aren't as good as the rest at certain games. And don't force anyone to play who doesn't want to. Have alternatives, such as coloring books or cards, available. Plan more games than you think you will need for the time allowed, but don't feel that you have to play all of the games. If any game drags or is obviously not being enjoyed, drop it and go to another.

Animal Crackers

Write the names of common zoo animals on bits of paper and have each child draw one. Arrange chairs in a circle, one fewer than there are children. One of the children starts out as the "animal trainer." He or she walks slowly around the circle, calling out names of animals, one at a time. As an animal is called, the child who drew that name gets up and follows the animal trainer around the circle. At any time, the animal trainer may call out, "animal crackers." At that time, all the children, including the animal trainer, try to sit in the vacant chairs. The child left without a chair becomes the new animal trainer.

Arm Wrestling

This is best played by closely matched children and kept in the spirit of fun, not full competition. Players sit across the table from one another, place their right elbows on the table, and clasp hands. At a given signal, each tries to push the other's hand down to touch the table. For less competitive variations, see Thumb Wrestling, Hand Wrestling, and One-Legged Hand Wrestling below.

Balloon Ball

This is volleyball played with a balloon. It can even be played indoors if you have a large enough room, with nothing breakable in the immediate area. Tie a string or rope across the playing area, about a foot higher than the average height of the children. Divide the children into two teams and place them on opposite sides of the string. The "ball" is served by tossing it across the "net." Once in motion, the balloon can only be hit with the open hand, and a player may not hit the balloon twice in a row. If the balloon touches the ground on one side of the string, the other team gets a point. The team on whose side the balloon hit the ground starts the game again by tossing the balloon over the string. The first team to get twenty-one points is the winner.

Balloon Break I

Each child has a blown-up balloon tied to one or both ankles. The children then try to break each others balloons while protecting their own. This game is best played outside, preferably without shoes.

Balloon Break II

This is a variation on the Mexican piñata. It is an outdoor summer game, best played when the children are in swimsuits. Fill a number of large balloons with water and hang them from a tree or from anything else handy. One at a time, blindfold each child, give him a stick, turn him around several times, and let him try several times to hit a balloon. A successful hit wins a cooling shower and a prize.

Balloon Races

Each child is given a blown-up balloon, and each must try to get it across the finish line following the rules. Variations include holding the balloon between the knees, kicking it ahead as you walk, blowing it without touching it, and pushing it with your nose while crawling.

Balloon Toss

This is strictly an outdoor game. Form two teams, and have the teams line up facing each other. The members of a team should be in a straight line, far enough apart so that they cannot touch one another.

Have a supply of water balloons for each team. The first child for each team picks up a water balloon and tosses it to the next child. The balloon is tossed down the line until it breaks or reaches the last child, who puts it on the ground. The team with the most unbroken balloons wins.

Beanbag Toss

This game can be played using beanbags you buy or make in advance, or those made by the children at the party (see the section on Arts and Crafts). The game simply involves having a child stand in a marked spot and try to hit a target with the beanbag. The target can be a basket, a large pot, a hole in a box, a pie tin hanging from a tree branch, or anything else you can think of.

Blind Man's Bluff

This game is best played with a large group of children. One child is "it," and is blindfolded. The rest of the children hold hands and form a circle around the "blind man." The blind man claps once, and the circle begins to move. When the blind man claps again, the circle stops. The blind man then points to one child and gets one guess as to who it is. If the blind man is right, then that child becomes the next blind man.

If the guess is wrong, the chosen child must come into the circle with the blind man. With both of them staying in the circle, the blind man tries to tag the other child. Once tagged, the child must stand still. The blind man can then touch the child in an attempt to learn who it is. If the blind man guesses correctly, the chosen child becomes the next blind man. If the blind man cannot tag or identify the chosen child in a limited time, he or she must repeat as blind man.

In a variation on this game, when the circle stops, the blind man points to one child and gives a command requiring use of the voice, such as "Cry like a baby," or "Howl like a coyote." If the blind man can't guess correctly, the circle moves again and the blind man makes another try.

Bobbing for Apples

This is traditionally a Halloween game, but it's fun at any time. Ideally, the game should be played with a large tub. It should always be played where some water on the floor will not do any damage. Outdoors is best, or in a garage. Fill the tub (or pail or sink) with water, and place a number of apples in the water.

The children should also be wearing clothes that will not be damaged by water. As a precaution, you may want to slip a waterproof windbreaker on each child as his or her turn comes up. The children kneel by the tub, hold their hands behind their backs, and try to get an apple out of the water using only their teeth.

Bottle Ring

Make a ring with an opening about two inches across. Cut it out of light wood, heavy cardboard, or a plastic coffee can lid. With a piece of string about two feet long, tie the ring to a stick several feet long. Have each child hold the end of the stick and try to loop the ring over the neck of a pop bottle within a limited time. To maintain interest, make up as many of these rings as possible, so that many children can play at once. As a variation, use full bottles of soda. Each child plays until he or she rings a bottle, and then gets to drink it. (Limit one bottle of soda per child.)

Box Relay

Divide the children into two teams. Have a set of boxes for each team, each set having the same number of different sized boxes, one nestled inside the other. The first member of each team runs to the boxes and takes them apart, holds up the smallest box, and then puts the boxes back together. The child then runs back to the team and tags the next team member, who repeats the action. The first team to have all of its members take the boxes apart and put them back together is the winner.

Capture the Flag

This game is best played with a lot of players (eight to ten or more) and a lot of room. Mark off the boundaries of a playing area, rectangular and as large as possible, as well as a center line. Divide the children into two teams. The game can be played with one flag (handkerchief, scarf, etc.) per team, or one per player.

The flag or flags are placed on the ground at each end of the playing area. The idea is to grab the opponent's flag without being tagged by one of the opposite team members. If a child is tagged in "enemy territory," he or she must stand outside the playing area behind the enemy's end of the field. One variation is that once a child captures a flag, he cannot be captured while returning to his own end of the field. A player may also free one of his own captured teammates by tagging the prisoner without being tagged by the enemy. A player cannot free a prisoner and capture a flag on the same trip into enemy territory, nor can he capture more than one flag on a given trip. The first team to capture the enemy's flag (or all of the flags) is the winner. You may want to put a time limit on the game, declaring the team with the most flags at the end of the period to be the winner.

Categories

This is a game for four or more players, best played by older children. With the children contributing ideas, make up a list of about twenty categories (states, sports, car models, etc.). Have each child in turn pick one category. All of the children write the chosen categories on their paper. (If there are five children, they would end up with five categories.)

To start the first round, a player chosen at random picks a letter of the alphabet at random. The children then have a limited period of time to write down as many items in each of their categories starting with that letter. (For example, if the letter is "T," and the first category is "cars," answers would include "Tempo" and "Taurus." If another category is "states," answers would include "Texas" and "Tennessee.") After the time is up, trade papers and score them. There is one point for a correct answer, and two points for a correct answer that no one else thought of. After a predetermined number of rounds, the one with the highest score is the winner.

Charades

Divide the children into two teams. Have a list of cha-rades ready, or have each child make up one before the game starts. Write them on pieces of paper, fold them, and put them in a bowl. For younger children, use single words, such as the names of animals, household items, and so on. For older children, use current movies or songs, book titles, etc. Alternating teams, each child in turn must take a charade from the bowl and act it out for his or her team. Put a time limit on each charade. The team that guesses the most correctly wins.

Close the Gap

This game requires a lot of room (outdoors) and is best with a large group of children. Two children are chosen as the "chaser" and the "chased." The rest of the children stand in a large circle, just far enough apart so that each can join hands with the child on either side.

At the signal to start, the chaser starts after the chased child. The chased child weaves in and out of the circle. Every time that he or she enters the circle between two children, those two children join hands. Now, neither the chaser nor the chased child can go between those two children for the rest of the game. The object of the game for the chased child is to close all the gaps in the circle, ending up inside the circle while the chaser is on the outside. The chaser tries to tag the chased child before the circle is closed.

Cops and Robbers

This is a team version of hide-and-seek. The "cops" cover their eyes and count to 50 or 100 while the "robbers" run off and hide. Then the cops go off in search of the robbers. A robber who is tagged by a cop is taken back to home base or jail. Another robber can free a captured robber by tagging him at the jail before he himself is tagged by a cop. If one robber frees another, both are out for the rest of the game, and cannot be recaptured. After all the robbers are caught or freed, the score for the cop team is the total number of robbers caught but not freed. The teams then switch roles. After two games, the team that scored the highest number of points as cops is the winner.

Cowboys and Indians

This game requires a lot of room, and is best played with a lot of children. At the start of the game, all the children are "Indians." The children stand in a circle, about five feet apart, and facing in a clockwise direction. You, or one of the children, act as the "leader." At the leader's signal, a shout or a whistle, the Indians begin running in a circle. Each child tries to tag the child in front before being tagged by the child behind.

After ten or twenty seconds, the signal to stop is given. Any tagged Indian now becomes a "cowboy," and moves to the center of the circle. The circle spreads out, the signal is given again, and the chase begins. Start and stop the circle occasionally, and change the direction of the circle from time to time. The last Indian left is the winner.

Dodge Ball

This can be played indoors with a balloon or a wadded-up sheet of paper, or outdoors with a beach ball. The players form a circle, with one player in the center. The others try to hit the one in the center with the ball. If the child in the center is hit, the one who hit him takes his place in the center.

Drop the Clothespin

This is an old game, involving a household item most children have probably never seen. Substitute coins, candy, or other small items for clothespins if necessary. Have each child kneel on a chair and drop the items over the shoulder into a basket or large pot. The child with the most clothespins in the target wins. As an alternative, when using coins or candy, the child gets to keep everything that goes into the basket.

Drop the Hanky

This is a good game for a large group of children, best in the four-to-seven-year range. One child is "it," and the rest form a large circle, facing inward. The child who is "it" holds a handkerchief and walks slowly around the outside of the circle. The children in the circle chant the old song:

A tisket, a tasket, a green and yellow basket,
I wrote a letter to my love, and on the way I dropped it.
I dropped it, I dropped it, the green and yellow basket,
A little child picked it up and put it in his pocket.

At any time, the child who is "it" may drop the hanky behind any child in the circle. "It" then takes off running, and the child by the hanky tries to catch "it" before he or she makes it all the way around the circle and takes the vacated place in the circle. If "it" is tagged, he or she is "it" again. If not, the child left out of the circle is "it" for the next round.

Ducks and Geese

This game is played outdoors, with a large flat area, and is best with a large number of children. One player is "it," and the others sit on the ground in a large circle. The child who is "it" walks around the outside of the circle, tapping each child on the head and saying either "duck" or "goose." If the tapped child is called a duck, nothing happens. If the child who is "it" says "goose," the "goose" jumps up and chases "it" around the outside of the circle, trying to tag him before he gets back and sits in the space vacated by the "goose." If "it" makes it back without being tagged, then the goose is "it" for the next game.

Find the Button

Pass a piece of heavy string or twine through a button or washer and tie the string in a circle large enough for all the children to sit around and hold on to with both hands. One child is "it," and stands outside the circle. All of the children keep their hands moving on the string to confuse the one who is "it," while the button is passed from hand to hand. If the one who is "it" finds the button, the child caught with it is now "it."

Find the Leader

The child who is "it" leaves the room for a moment, while a leader for the rest of the group is selected. When the first child returns, the leader starts various motions, tapping his head or scratching his elbow, without letting on that he is the leader, and the rest of the children follow. The one who is it must figure out who the leader is. If the leader is discovered within a time limit, then he is "it."

Firefighter's Race

This is a variation on relay races. Divide the children into two or more teams, giving each team a small glass or paper cup to carry water. Start each team with a full glass of water. The first member for each team runs to the other end of the yard and dumps the water into the team's bucket or other container (make sure that all the containers are the same size). He or she then returns to the starting line and hands the glass to the next team member, who fills the glass from a common water source or (for a lot of fun and a big mess) with a garden hose. The first team to fill its bucket is the winner.

Follow the Leader

This is a good game for younger children, providing lots of fun and not requiring exceptional athletic ability. It is best played outdoors, where there is lots of room and there are few things to break.

A leader is selected, usually at random. The leader starts out and the rest of the children follow in a line. The leader tries to do various things that the others will not be able to follow. These can include jumping over small objects, hopping on one foot for a distance, climbing over a fence, etc.

Players who fail to follow the leader can be made to drop out, but the game can also be played just for fun, with frequent changes of leader.

Gossip

All of the children sit in a circle. Give the first child a sheet of paper with a sentence written on it, or whisper the sentence in the child's ear if he is too young to read well. The first child then whispers the sentence in the ear of the next child, and so on, around the circle. The last child repeats the sentence aloud, after which you read the original sentence. The results will usually be highly garbled.

Ha, Ha, Ha

This is a simple game with few rules and no real losers. The object of the game is to keep from laughing. The children sit or stand in a circle, and one child begins by saying "Ha," as seriously as possible. The next child must say "Ha, Ha," the third child says "Ha, Ha, Ha," and so on, around the circle. Any child who laughs or says the wrong number of "Ha's" drops out of the circle. The drop-outs can do anything they want to try to make those still in the circle laugh, except touch them. The last one to laugh is the winner.

Hand Wrestling

The players stand facing each other with feet apart and right feet touching, and grasp right hands. At a given signal, they push or pull at each other, trying to make one another lose balance. The first to move a foot is the loser.

Hands Up

This game is best played with at least eight players, and the only equipment needed is a quarter (or perhaps a smaller coin for smaller children). Divide the children into two teams, and have them sit on opposite sides of a long table. (If there aren't enough chairs, only one team really needs to sit at a time.)

One team, sitting in a row, starts with the quarter, passing it from member to member under the table. The leader of the other team counts slowly to ten (not necessarily aloud) and says, "Hands up." The players on the team with the quarter immediately raise their closed fists above the table. When the other leader says "Hands down," the team members slap their open hands down on the table, one of them slapping down the quarter and covering it with his or her hand.

The members of the other team now confer, trying to guess which player at the table has the quarter. If the guess is correct, the quarter changes sides. If not, the quarter stays for another round. The winning team is the one with the most correct guesses after a given time limit or a given number of rounds.

Hat Toss

There are many variations on the simple game of tossing things into a hat. Give each child five playing cards, crumpled sheets of paper, peanuts in the shell, soda straws, or anything else on hand. Have them stand behind a line and see who can get the most into the target.

Hide-and-Seek

This is a well known game with many variations. The basic idea of the game is that one person is "it," the others run off and hide, and "it" tries to find and tag them before they can get back to home base.

Generally, "it" stands at home base with his eyes covered and counts to 50 or 100 while everyone else hides. "It" then calls out, "Ready or not, here I come." The child who is "it" then tries to find and tag the others before they can touch home base. Players can stay hidden, or can make a run for home as soon as they think that they can make it without being tagged. Anyone tagged by "it" is a prisoner, but can be freed by another player who makes it to home base and calls out "Home free." If the last child in frees any remaining prisoners, then "it" is "it" again. If "it" captures the rest, the first one tagged is "it" for the next game.

Horse

Horse is a basketball shooting contest that can be played by two or more. All that is needed is a basketball and a hoop. The first player attempts a shot from anywhere on the court. It can be a simple set shot, a jump shot, a hook shot, or whatever the player wants to do. If the first player makes the shot, the rest of the players in turn must make the identical shot. Anyone missing the shot is assigned the letter "H." When someone misses their second shot, they are assigned an "O," then an "R," then an "S," then an "E." The game can go until the first player gets "HORSE," or until only one is left. If the first player misses the first shot, the lead passes down the line in rotation.

Hot Potato

Traditionally played with an actual potato, this game can be played with a small beach ball, a tennis ball, a softball, or anything similar in size. The players sit on the ground in a circle, with the child who is "it" seated in the middle of the circle. "It" tosses the potato to one of the children in the circle and closes his eyes. The children toss the potato at random to others in the circle, getting rid of it as quickly as possible (as if it were, indeed, a hot potato). At any point, "it" opens his eyes and calls out, "hot potato." Whoever is holding the potato at that time is out of the game. The last one out is the winner.

Ice Cube Relay

Play this game outdoors with a large group, preferably on a warm day. Divide the children into teams and give each team an ice cube. (Make sure that the ice cubes are as nearly the same size as possible.) The object of the game is to melt the ice cube. The ice cube must be passed from team member to team member every few seconds. Players can rub the ice cube with their hands or against their clothes, or against each other, but they cannot put it in their mouths and it cannot touch the ground. The first team to melt their ice cube is the winner.

Johnny-Jump-Up

This is a simpler but more active version of Simon Says, easier to play, and more fun for smaller children. The children can play it individually or as teams. The children pretend to be flower seeds, waiting for a signal from spring that it is time to grow.

One player is "Spring," and the others are seeds. The seeds count off, alternating as a "number one" or a "number two." They then spread out and crouch down, waiting to sprout. Spring claps hands once, twice, or three times. If there is one clap, all the number ones jump up, if two claps, all the number twos jump up. On three claps, all the seeds jump up. Any seed jumping up at the wrong time, or failing to jump at the right time, is out.

Memory Test

Place a number of small, everyday items on a tray, covering them with a towel. Have the children sit around the tray and remove the towel for a few moments. Cover the tray and remove it. Have younger children draw pictures of as many things on the tray as they can remember. Have older children list the items on a sheet of paper.

Mother May I?

One child acts as "Mother," while the rest line up on the starting line. Mother goes down the line, telling each child to take one, two or three giant steps or baby steps, or hops, or whatever. The child called upon must ask "Mother, may I?" and receive the answer, "Yes, you may," before moving. If the child moves without such permission, he must go back to the starting line and start over. The first child to reach Mother becomes the new Mother.

Musical Chairs I

Place a number of chairs in a circle facing out, using one fewer chair than there are children. Play a song on a stereo or radio while the children walk around the ring of chairs. When you turn off the music, each child must sit in a chair. The one who didn't get a chair is out of this round. Remove a chair, and repeat until there is one child in the last chair.

Musical Chairs II

Play as above, but, when the music stops, a child without a chair can sit in another child's lap. Remove a chair and repeat. Keep playing until all the children are sitting in the same chair, if they can get that far without total chaos.

Musical Package

Place a toy or other prize in a small box. Put that box in a larger box, and that in a box that is larger still. Use as many boxes as you wish (or use multiple layers of wrapping paper). Have the children sit in a circle on the floor and pass the package around the circle while music is played. When the music stops, whoever is holding the package opens one box or layer of wrapping. Whoever gets to the actual prize gets to keep it.

Odds and Evens

This is a game played with the hands, similar to "Rock, Paper, Scissors," played by two players. One player is designated as "odd," and the other as "even." At the count of three, each player holds out his or her right hand, showing from zero (closed fist) to five fingers. The total number of fingers shown by the two players is added together. If the total is odd, the "odd" player gets a point; if the total is even, the "even" player gets a point. Play a given number of rounds, or up to a certain point count (say ten points).

One-Legged Hand Wrestling

The players stand facing each other and grasp right hands. Each reaches down with the left hand and grasps his own left ankle. The players then try to make each other lose balance. The first to fall or to let go of the left ankle is the loser.

Orchestra

Another game similar to "Simon Says." Each child chooses a musical instrument to pretend to play. The game is best played if only one or two children pick the same instrument. One child acts as the conductor of the orchestra, and begins making the motions of playing his or her instrument (swinging arms up and down for a drum, puffing cheeks for a horn, etc.). The others follow by pretending to play their instruments, keeping an eye on the conductor. At any time, the conductor may "switch" instruments, going through the motions of playing an instrument picked by another child. The child "playing" that instrument must now stop playing and puts his hands over his ears. All the other children must also "switch" to the instrument the conductor is now playing. When the conductor returns to his original instrument, all the children return to theirs. The conductor switches at will, going from the original instrument to someone else's, and then back to the original. Any child caught not making the proper move (either changing instruments or covering the ears) drops out of the game. The last one left is the winner, and the conductor for the next game.

Peanut Toss

A simple game with dozens of variations, easy to customize for a theme party. The children toss peanuts, buttons, coins, marbles, or anything on hand at a target. The target can be a box, a bucket, a large, empty can, a target painted on an old sheet, or anything else you can think of. Targets that are smaller and/or farther away are worth more points.

Pin the Tail on the Donkey

This can also be played as pin the "something" on the "anything." Make up something current or with local significance or interest. Pin the sword on the Ninja Turtle or pin the hat on the ballplayer. Especially for younger children, don't actually use pins. Use a loop of tape or a small ball of play dough for sticking purposes. To maintain interest, have more than one target, and more than one child playing at once. Have each child's name prewritten on the tail or other item. Don't put the blindfold on too tightly, especially for younger children, and don't spin them around more than once or twice.

Pom-Pom Pull Away

This game should be played outside, with a large number of children and a good-sized, open space. Designate a square playing area about twenty-five feet on a side. One child, who is "it," stands in the area, while all the rest line up on one side of the square. The child who is "it" calls out, "Pom-pom pull away, run away, run away," and all the children must run across the square, trying to get to the opposite side without being tagged. Anyone tagged must join "it" in the center of the square and help tag the others on the next run through. Each time, those in the center call out the rhyme in unison. The last child not tagged is the winner, and is "it" for the next game.

Poor Loser

This is a variation on the standard foot race, best played outdoors with a large group. Establish a starting line, a finish line, and out-of-bounds lines on the sides. The children line up at the starting line and race for the finish. The last place finisher is out of the race and the rest run another race, starting at the original finish line and racing to the original start line. The child who was out after the first lap gets to stand in the race course and interfere with runners or push them out of bounds. The last child in the second lap also drops out and joins the first loser in the middle. Any children who steps out of bounds also joins the group in the middle. Repeat the races until there is only one child left.

Red Rover

This can be played on a large lawn, and is best with a large group of children. Divide the children into two teams, and have the teams line up facing each other, about ten feet apart. One team holds hands and the team captain calls out, "Red Rover, Red Rover, let _____ come over," naming one member of the other team. The player whose name was called runs across the open space and tries to break through the line by running into the joined hands of any two players. If the player does break through, he picks one of the two players between whom he broke through to go back with him to his own team. If he does not break through, he stays and joins the other team.

Relay Races

Start by dividing the children into two or more groups, trying to maintain a balance of athletic ability between the groups. The common thread in relay races is that the first child in each group races to a point and returns, usually performing some task en route (such as holding an egg in a spoon) or doing something at the far point (such as putting on a jacket and taking it off). On completing the course, the first child tags the second child on the team, who repeats the actions. The first team to have all of its members complete the course wins.

One variation of the relay race is to have a bucket of water at the start and a small empty glass at the far point. Each child in turn takes a tablespoon of water from the bucket and dumps it in the glass. The first team to fill the glass wins. Do not try this in your home.

Another variation is the balloon basketball relay. Divide the children into two or more teams. Each team has a balloon, and a basket at the other end of the room or yard. The first player from each team hits the balloon into the air, and continues to keep it in the air until it goes into the basket. The balloon can not be caught or allowed to touch the floor. If either happens, the player goes back and starts over. Once the balloon is in the basket, the player takes it out and carries it back to the next player on the team. The first team to have each player make a basket is the winner.

Ring Toss

Make rings by cutting out strips of cardboard, pasting the ends together, and wrapping with ribbon or wrapping paper. Or have the children do this as a preliminary activity. Set up a row of empty pop bottles and let the children try to throw the rings over the necks of the bottles. A variation of this is to use full soda bottles, or a mixture of full and empty bottles. When children ring a full bottle, they get to drink it. (Limit one bottle of soda per child.)

Ring-a-Levio

This is a team version of hide-and-seek, and requires a large area with a lot of places to hide. The children are divided into two teams, and a base area or "jail" about five feet square is marked off, together with a "danger area" about ten feet square. One team stands in the jail while the second team runs off and hides. When the leader of the hiding team calls out, "Ready," the members of the first team go out to look for them. The leader of the first team stays in the jail. As members of the second team are found and tagged, they are brought back to the jail, where they must remain unless freed.

The leader of the first team stays in the jail to guard the prisoners. A member of the second team can free one prisoner at a time by jumping into the jail, crying out, "Ring-a-Levio," and running away. The leader of the first team can recapture either or both of them by tagging them before they get out of the danger area. If all the members of the second team are captured within a time limit, they are the losers. The teams then switch roles for another game.

Rock, Paper, Scissors

This is an age old game for two players, requiring no equipment. Each player, on the count of three, holds out a hand in the form of a rock (fist), paper (open palm), or scissors (first two fingers extended in a "V"). The winner is determined by the combination of choices. Scissors cut (beat) paper, paper wraps rock, and rock smashes scissors. Award one point for each victory, with the first player to reach a certain number of points the winner.

Run for Your Supper

This game is best played outside with a lot of players and a lot of room. All the players form a circle, holding hands, except the one player who is "it." "It" walks around the circle and stops anywhere he wants, pulling the hands of two adjacent children apart, saying "Run for your supper." The two children run around the circle in opposite directions, while "it" takes the place of one of them. The first child back to the gap completes the circle, and the other one becomes "it."

Sardines

This is a kind of reverse version of "Hide-and-Seek." All the players stand with their eyes closed and count while the one who is "it" goes off to hide. After a given period of time, a second player goes off in search of the first. If the second player doesn't find the first within one minute, he or she is out of the game. If the second player does find the first, he or she joins the first player in the hiding place. The action is repeated by the other players, one at a time, until the last player is out or finds the rest of them hiding, all in the same place (and trying not to laugh).

Scavenger Hunt

Divide the children into teams, and give each team a list of things to find. This is best played outside, as there will be a lot of running around and a lot of confusion. Played outside, the list can include natural items like a stone or a piece of bark.

A variation on this is the magazine scavenger hunt. Give each child (or team) a list of common things, such as a car, a house, a TV, and so on. Place a stack of old magazines in the center of the floor, and have the children try to find pictures of the things on the list.

Secret Mission

Divide the children into two groups. Give each group a sealed envelope with clues for finding the next envelope, and so on. (Each group has an entirely different set of envelopes and clues.) For smaller children, everything can take place in the house or yard. For older children, hide the envelopes around the neighborhood, with the last clue bringing them back to the house.

Shopping

Place a large number of boxes and cans on a table, marking each with a real or made-up price. The prices should be large and easy to read. One at a time, give the children shopping bags and let them fill the bags with as many items as they can in a very short, closely timed period (say, ten to fifteen seconds). After each turn, add up the prices of the items in the bag, write it down, and return the items to the table. The child with the highest dollar total of groceries is the winner.

Simon Says

This game is something like "Mother May I?" One child starts out as "Simon," and the rest stand in a line. If Simon says, "Simon says, touch your ears," then everyone must touch their ears. If someone doesn't touch his ears, he is out of the game. If Simon just says, "Touch your ears," anyone touching his or her ears is out of the game. The last one left wins.

Sort the Mail

Have a number of post cards, or post-card-sized pieces of cardboard, each with the name of a major city written on it. Have a number of boxes, each with a city name clearly printed on the side. Each child is given a stack of ten post cards. Standing behind a line, the child tries to toss the post card into the correct box. A post card in the right box earns ten points, in the wrong box, minus five points, and on the floor, no points. Experiment to see how far from the boxes the children should stand while making their tosses.

Spin the Bottle

Prepare a supply of notes listing tasks or actions to be performed. These should be fun things, but not embarrassing; for example, "Pat your head and rub your tummy at the same time," or "Act like (an animal)," to be pictured on the note. Have the children sit in a circle on the floor. Roll up a note, stick it in the neck of the bottle, and spin the bottle on the floor in the center of the circle. When the bottle stops spinning, the child it points to must do whatever the note says.

Spud

This game is played with a large group and a ball soft enough to throw at other players. Use a small inflatable ball or a sponge rubber ball. All the players stand in a close group while one of the players throws the ball straight up in the air and calls out the name of one of the other players. The named player stays to catch the ball while the other players take off running. When the named player catches the ball, he yells out, "Freeze," and all the others must freeze in their tracks. The player with the ball then throws it at any of the other players. If the player is hit, that player gets assigned the letter "S." When a player gets hit a second time during the course of the game, he gets the letter "P," and then "U," and finally, "D." When a player picks up all four letters, he or she is out of the game.

If the player throwing the ball doesn't hit anyone, that player picks up a letter. If a player is hit, he or she gets to pick up the ball and throw it at another player. If a player is thrown at and missed, that player picks up the ball, throws it in the air, and calls out a new name.

Play the game until the first player is out with S-P-U-D, or until all are out but one.

Statues

A starting line and a finish line are established (about fifty feet apart), and the child who is "it" stands at the finish line. The rest of the children line up at the starting line. The one who is "it" turns his back on the rest and starts counting aloud, in a regular cadence, to five. During the count, the other children move as quickly as they dare toward the finish line. At the count of five, "it" turns around. All the children must be totally motionless at this point. If "it" sees anyone moving, that child must go back to the starting line. The first child to the finish line is "it" for the next game.

Steal the Bacon

This is a good team game for a large group, without complicated rules. It can be played in an average-sized backyard. Divide the children into two teams of exactly the same number. If there is one child left over, he serves as referee. If not, you are the referee.

Mark off two parallel lines about fifteen to twenty feet apart. Have the teams line up along the lines, and have each team count off from their left to right. (This way, the children who are "number one" on each team will be at opposite ends of the lines.) The referee puts the "bacon" (a ball, a hat, or a small cardboard box) in the center of the playing area. The referee then gets out of the way and calls out a number between one and the number of players on each team.

The player on each team who counted out that number tries to steal the bacon and get back across his or her team line without being tagged by the opposite team member. If the player makes it across the line, his team gets a point. If the player is tagged before reaching the line, there is no point for that round. In either case, the referee puts the bacon back in the center and calls out another number. The first team to score twenty-five points wins.

Suitcase Relay Race

Divide the children into two or more teams. For each team, have a suitcase containing a shirt, a pair of pants, a hat, and a pair of shoes (the larger the better for all of these items). At the signal, the first member of each team runs to the suitcase, puts on the clothes, claps hands, takes off the clothes, puts them back in the suitcase, closes it, and returns to the team. The rest of the team members repeat the sequence, one at a time. The first team to have all members complete the routine wins.

Tag

There are endless variations on the game of tag. The basics of the game are that the child who is "it" must tag or touch one of the other children. The others can avoid being tagged by running away, hiding, or in some way being "safe." Being safe can involve touching a designated home base, not moving, standing on one foot, and so on.

Ball tag: Players are tagged by being hit with a soft ball, such as a beach ball, rather than actually being touched by the child who is "it."

Freeze tag: A child who is tagged must remain frozen to the spot, unless he or she is tagged by one of the others who have not been frozen. The child who is "it" wins if he or she can freeze all the other children.

Monster tag: The child who is "it" is a monster. As he tags other children, they become monsters too, and help chase after the children who have not been tagged. The last one tagged is the winner, and the first one tagged becomes the monster for the next game.

Piggy-back tag: Players can save themselves from being tagged by one riding another piggy-back. They have to separate when the child who is "it" gets ten feet away from them, and the same two players cannot piggy-back twice in a row.

Prayer tag: A child is safe from being tagged by "it" if he or she can kneel down with hands clasped as if in prayer before being tagged. After "it" gets at least ten feet away, the child must get back up again.

Skunk tag: A child can't be tagged if he or she puts an

arm under a knee, holds the nose, and hops ten steps. After ten steps, the child must start running again.

Spot tag: The child who is tagged must hold the tagged spot with one hand while trying to tag someone else with the free hand.

Thumb Wrestling

The players sit paired across from one another at a table. Each places his right hand on the table, with the little finger touching the table and the thumb up in the air. The players curl their fingers into a hook, and link hands. At the count of three, the players each try to pin the other's thumb down to the top of the hand.

Treasure Hunts

There are hundreds of possible variations on a treasure hunt, tailoring the game to the ages and abilities of the children at the party. For younger children, simply hide the treasure (coins, goodies, small toys, etc.) around the room, the house, or the yard. Numerous small prizes can be hidden in a sandbox or in a pile of leaves. Make sure that there are plenty of prizes to go around, and that each child get something. For a theme party, hide treats or paper cutouts related to the theme.

For older children, you can add oral or written clues. Or, have a list of clues for each child, with a prize for each to be found.

One variation is to give each child a similar kind of magazine and a pair of scissors. Name a common thing, such as a car or a house, and see who can cut out the most pictures of that thing within a specified time. Or, have them look for and cut out pictures of things that start with a "B," or a "Q," or any letter.

Tug-of-War

This game should be played outside, and requires a long, sturdy rope. Either divide the children randomly into two teams, or have two "captains" choose sides. Mark off a center line, tie a rag to the center of the rope, and hold the rag over the center line. Have team members spread out along their end of the rope and grasp it firmly. At a given signal, the teams begin pulling. The object of the game is to pull the first member of the opposing team across the center line.

Twenty Questions

This can be played by a small group playing individually, or you can divide the children into teams. One person thinks of a thing and announces only that it is "animal," "vegetable," or "mineral." (Animal includes human, and mineral is the all-other category.) The other players ask questions about the thing which can be answered "yes" or "no." Keep track of the number of questions. If no one guesses right within twenty questions, the person (or team) who came up with the thing wins, and gets to go again.

Wheelbarrow Races

This is best played outside, where there is plenty of room, and no furniture to be run into. The children are divided into teams of two. One member of each team walks upright, holding up the feet of the other team member, who walks on his hands. When the team reaches the halfway mark, they switch positions and return to the finish line.

Wrong-Handed Toss

This is a good game for older children, as it tends to equalize any athletic talents and lets girls and boys compete on an equal basis. The game can be played as a variation of beanbag toss or hat toss. Other options include throwing snowballs or baseballs at a target, shooting baskets, throwing a football at a hanging tire, and so on. The only change is that right-handers must throw with the left hand, and vice versa.

Paper and Pencil Games

Hangman

This is best played in groups of two. One child starts the game as the "hangman." He draws a scaffold and a noose, picks a secret word with up to seven letters, and draws a blank line for each letter in the word. The other child then names a letter he thinks is in the word. If the letter is actually in the word, the hangman fills in the appropriate blank or blanks. If the letter is not in the word, the hangman draws a head at the end of the noose. With each additional wrong letter, the hangman draws the neck, the body, the two arms, and the two legs of the hanged man. If the second child guesses the word before the hanged man is completed, he wins, and becomes the hangman for the next game. If not, the hangman wins.

Squares

On a sheet of paper, draw seven rows of seven dots each, in a grid pattern. Two players alternate, drawing a line between two adjacent dots. (Up and down or side by side, but not diagonally.) If a drawn line completes a square, the child drawing that fourth side puts his initial in the completed square, and he gets another turn. When all squares have been completed, the initials are counted and the child with the most wins.

Word Search

Give each child a pencil and a sheet of paper. Pick an appropriate long word, such as "birthday" or "Halloween," and have each child write down as many words as possible made up of the letters of that word. Whoever comes up with the most words within the time limit wins.

Card and Dice Games

Cheater

This game is played with a regular deck of cards, and can be played by three or more players. Deal out as many of the cards as possible so that each child gets the same number of cards. Place the rest of the deck facedown in the middle of the table. The player to the left of the dealer takes any card from his hand, puts it facedown on the deck in the middle of the table, and announces the value of the card (King, Seven, etc.). The next player must place any card from his hand face down on the deck and announce that it is the next higher card. (The next card after a King is played is an Ace, followed by a Two.) If anyone doubts that the card played was in fact what it was supposed to be, he calls out "Cheater!" The card is then turned faceup. If the card is what it was claimed to be, the challenger must pick up all the cards in the middle of the table and put them in his hand. If the card was not what it was supposed to be, the child who played the card must pick up all the cards. The first one to get rid of all the cards in his hand is the winner.

Concentration

An entire deck of cards is placed facedown on a table so that the cards do not overlap. Each player in turn can turn up any two cards. If the two cards make a pair, the player keeps the two cards and takes another turn. If the cards do not match, they are turned back down and the next player takes a turn. Every time a card is turned up and then turned back over, the players must try to remember which card is where. When all the cards have been picked up, the player with the most cards is the winner.

Crazy Eights

This game can be played by three or more players, using a regular deck of playing cards. Deal seven cards to each child, placing the rest of the deck facedown in the middle of the table. The player to the dealer's left starts by placing any card faceup in the middle, next to the deck. The next player plays either a card of the same suit or of the same value. Eights are wild, and can be played at any time. The child playing an Eight must then announce which suit is to be played next.

If a child cannot play a card from his hand, he must draw the top card from the deck. If that card cannot be played, the child continues drawing until he can play a card. If a child cannot play a card and there are no cards left in the deck, play passes to the next child. The first child to get rid of all of his or her cards is the winner.

Go Fish

This game is usually played with four players, although anywhere from two to six can play. If there are two or three players, each is dealt six cards. For up to six players, deal five cards each. The remaining cards are placed in the center of the table, facedown. Some people play with these cards in a stack, some spread them out.

The object of the game is to get the most sets of four-of-a-kind. The first player asks any other player for a particular card, such as a Jack. If the asked player has any Jacks, he must give them all to the first player, who then gets another turn. If he has no Jacks, he says, "Go fish."

The first player then takes the top card from the stack or any card from the cards spread out in the middle of the table. If the chosen card in this case is a Jack, he shows it and takes another turn. If it is not the card he asked for, his turn is over.

Whenever a player gets all four of the same card, he takes them out of his hand and puts them on the table in front of him. When the cards in the middle are gone, the game continues without the fishing. When a player is out of cards, he gets no more turns for that game. The game is over when everyone is out of cards. The player with the most sets of four-of-a-kind is the winner.

Happy Families

This is a variation of "Go Fish." In this game, all the cards are dealt out. Players in turn ask one of the others for a particular card. If the asked player has the card, he must turn it (or them, if he has more than one) over to the child asking. The first child then gets to ask again. If the first child does get what he asks for, the turn passes to the next child. As the children get four-of-a-kind (a family), they lay them down in front of them. At the end of the game, the child with the most families is the winner.

Hearts

Hearts is played with three to six players, a regular deck of cards, and a pencil and paper to keep score. Deal out as many cards as possible so that each player gets the same number, placing any leftover cards in the center of the table. The player to the left of the dealer places any card faceup on the table. (Some play that whoever has the Two of Clubs starts by playing that card.) The other players follow, with each playing a card of the same suit. If a player does not have any card of that suit, he or she may play any card. The child playing the highest card of the proper suit wins that "trick," and picks up the cards and puts them facedown in front of him. This player then plays (leads) any card from his hand. A heart cannot be played on the first trick, and a heart cannot be led until someone has played a heart when he didn't have a card of the suit that was led. After all the cards have been played, each child counts up the number of hearts in the cards that he or she has taken. One point is scored for each heart taken, and the lowest score is the winner of the hand, and the dealer of the next hand. Play continues for a given number of rounds, or until someone reaches a certain number of points, such as 100. The child with the lowest score at that time is the winner.

A variation of hearts is to have the Queen of Hearts count as thirteen points, in addition to the regular one-point-per-heart. Another variation is to have each player look at his or her hand and pass three cards to the left before play begins. In another variation, if one player gets all thirteen hearts (and the Queen of Spades, if playing that variation also), then that player gets no points for the hand, and all the other players get thirteen points (or twenty-six points if playing with the Queen) apiece added to their scores.

I Doubt It

Three or more children can play this game. Deal out as many cards as possible so that all players get the same number of cards. Put any leftover cards in the center of the table.

The first player must put one to four cards in the center of the table, facedown, and announce that all the cards are aces. If this goes unchallenged, play continues, with the second player putting one to four cards down, and announcing that they are all Twos. Any player can challenge any play by saying, "I doubt it."

If a play is challenged, the cards just played are turned faceup. If these cards are in fact what the person said they were, the challenger must pick up all the cards that are in the center of the table. If the cards are not what they were claimed to be, then the person who was challenged must pick up all the cards in the center.

Even if a player has no Aces, or Twos, or whatever is required on his turn, he must put down at least one card and say that it is that card. The first player to get rid of all of his cards is the winner.

Mark Out

For this game you will need a pair of dice, and a pencil and paper for each player. Each child writes the numbers from one to twelve on his score card. The object of the game is to mark out all the numbers on the card. Numbers can be marked out two different ways. The first is to roll the dice and have the total match the number. For example, a child rolling a five and a six could mark out the eleven on his score card. The other way is to mark out one or both of the numbers rolled on the dice. In this case, a child rolling a five and a six could mark out both the five and the six. (If a child did roll a five and a six, for example, and the six had already been marked out, he could mark out the five.)

Each player throws the dice once for his or her turn. If no number can be marked out on that throw, the turn is over and the dice pass to the next player. The first player to mark out all twelve numbers is the winner.

Muggins

Muggins is played with a regular deck of cards, and requires four or more players. Deal four cards faceup in the center of the table, and deal out as many cards as possible so that each player has an equal number of cards. The players keep their cards facedown in a stack in front of them, and do not look at them. Place any remaining cards faceup on one of the cards in the center of the table.

The player to the dealer's left starts by turning over the top card in his or her stack. A card is played by placing it on a faceup card that is one value higher or lower. Thus, a Three can be played on a Two or on a Four. The exceptions are the King, which can only be played on a Queen, and the Ace, which can only be played on a Two.

If the first child cannot play the turned-up card, the card remains faceup in front of the child, and play proceeds to the left. For all turns after the first, the child whose turn it is may play on any face-up card on the table, whether it is in the center of the table or in front of one of the other players.

If it is possible on a turn to play a card in more than one place, an order must be followed. If possible, the card must be played in the center of the table. If that is not possible, then the child must play the card on the pile of the child closest to him on the left where it is possible to play.

The players have to watch for a play that is incorrect (such as an Ace played on a King, or a Six played on an Eight), or that doesn't follow the correct order (such as playing on another child's stack when the card could have been played in the middle). A child who spots a wrong play calls out "Muggins." The child who made the wrong play must then take the top card from the face-down pile of each of the other children.

If a child has turned over all of his face-down cards, he turns the face-up cards back down and continues play. The first one to get rid of all of his or her cards is the winner.

Neighbors

This game can be fun and different, because a player throwing the dice may score points for himself or for one of the other players, depending on the throw. The game can be played by two to six players, and requires three dice, and a pencil and paper for scoring.

Each player is assigned one or more numbers, depending on the number of players. If there are two players, one player is assigned the numbers one, two, and three, while the other is assigned four, five, and six. (What numbers are assigned is not important.) If there are three players, one player gets one and two, the second gets three and four, and the third gets five and six. For four or more players, each player gets one number, and any unassigned numbers are ignored.

To start, the first player rolls the three dice. Each number showing represents one point for the child assigned that number. For example, if the first roll showed a one, a two, and a four, the children assigned those numbers would get a point apiece, and no one else would get any points.

Either play to a certain number of points (twenty or

twenty-five), or play a certain number of rounds, with the highest score at the end being the winner.

A variation on the scoring is to use chips or coins instead of keeping score. Each child starts the game with a number of chips, say five or ten. For every "two" that is rolled, the child assigned the number two puts a chip into the center. The first child to get rid of all of his or her chips is the winner.

Old Maid

Old Maid is played with a regular deck of cards, and three or more players. To begin play, remove the Queen of Hearts from the deck and deal out all of the cards. (Don't worry if they don't come out even.) The children examine their cards, removing any pairs from their hands and placing the pairs facedown in front of them.

The player to the left of the dealer then pulls one card from the hand of the player to his or her right. If that card makes a pair in the child's hand, the pair is placed facedown on the table. The next child to the left then plays, and so on around the table. Play continues until all of the cards are paired up except the odd Queen. This is the "Old Maid," and the child left holding it loses the game.

Pig

This is a simple dice game that encourages children in learning to count and add. Any number can play, but the game goes best with three to four players. If there are more than that, divide the children into groups and have several games going at once.

The object of the game is to be the first to get 100 points. Each player in turn throws a single die one or more times. The player may throw them as many times as he or she wishes on any turn. The points are totaled following each throw, and are added to the player's score at the end of the turn, unless the player throws an Ace (a "one"). An Ace ends the turns and gives that player no points for that turn.

Rotation

This is a game of luck, playable by any number of children. You will need a pair of dice, and a pencil and paper for keeping score.

In the first round, each child gets one roll of the dice to try to roll a "two." Any child that does roll a two gets two points for that round. Any children not rolling a two get no points for the round. In the second round, each child gets one chance to roll a "three." Those succeeding get three points; the others get no points for the round.

After going through all the possible points, from two to twelve, the player with the highest total is the winner.

Rummy

Rummy is a good game for older children, teaching them the basics of card-playing and strategy. It is a good way to keep children entertained on a rainy afternoon, or for the last few guests staying late after the party.

Rummy can be played by two to six players. For two players, deal ten cards apiece; for three or four players, seven cards each; and for five or six players, six cards each. The rest of the deck is placed facedown in the center of the table, and the top card is turned up. The object of the game is to get rid of the cards in the hand by playing them (placing them faceup on the table) in groups. The groups can be three- or four-of-a-kind (for example, three Fours), or three or more in a row of the same suit (for example, the Three-Four-Five of Spades). The Ace is low, and can only be played at the low end of a sequence, such as Ace-Two-Three. Ace-King-Queen is not a valid play.

After the dealer turns up the top card of the deck, the player to the dealer's left begins. That player can either take the turned-up card or the top card in the face-down deck. If the player can play any cards (groups of three or more), he or she may do so at this time, or may chose to wait. During his or her turn, a player may also play on any groups that have already been played on the table. If three Fours are already on the table, for example, a player with the fourth Four may place it faceup on the table. The player concludes the turn by discarding any card on top of the face-up card in the center of the table.

The hand ends when one player plays all the cards in his or her hand. The winner is the player who "goes out." That player gets the total points of all the cards still held in the hands of the opponents. The points are counted as follows: face cards count ten points each, Aces count one point, and all other cards count as face value. The first player to get 100 or 200 points is the winner.

500 Rummy: This is a variation of Rummy, played by two to four players. For two players, deal thirteen cards each. For three or four players, deal seven cards. Play begins as in Rummy, but discards are spread out so that all cards in the discard pile can be seen, keeping them one on top of the other. The player whose turn it is can take the top card from the discard pile or take the top card from the deck without making a play or meld. The player may also take any other card from the discard pile, if he can make a play with it immediately. If taking a card from the discard pile other than the top card, the player must first show the other two (or more) cards that will be played with that card. In addition, the player must take all the other cards that are in the discard pile above that card and place those cards in his hand. If a player plays a single card on a group or meld already played by another player, he should be careful to keep that card in front of him.

The hand ends when one player goes out (that is, has no cards left). Each player then adds up the point total of the cards in front of him. Aces count fifteen points if played in a group of aces, but count one point if played in a sequence of Ace-Two-Three. Face cards count ten points, and all other cards count at face value. Each player then subtracts the value of the cards remaining in his or her hand. The total is added to (or subtracted from, if the points in a player's hand were more than the points on the table) the player's cumulative score, with the first player to reach 500 points declared the winner.

Other variations: There are many other variations on the game of Rummy, including, of course, Gin Rummy. These games can get very complicated, and the strategies are generally beyond the abilities of children (particularly Gin Rummy). The two variations discussed above should keep most children well entertained for an hour or two.

Slap Jack

This is a good card game for three or more players that relies more on reflexes than on card-playing ability. It is a good game for younger players. The players sit in a circle around a table or on the floor, where each can easily reach the center of the playing area.

The dealer deals out all the cards, and the player to the dealer's left places a card faceup in the center of the table. The children hold their cards facedown in a stack and do not look at them. Play continues to the left, with each child in turn placing a card faceup on top of the pile. Each card should be played as quickly as possible, and the child playing the card should let go of it without really seeing it until it hits the table.

When a Jack is turned up, the children try to slap the

card. The first child to slap the Jack picks up all the cards in the pile and adds them to his or her hand. If a child slaps a card that is not a Jack, that child must give his or her next card to the player who played the card that was slapped in error. Play continues until one player has all the cards.

Strike Three

This is a simple card game, and can be played by three or more children at a time. Sort through a deck of cards and take out as many sets of four-of-a-kind as there are children playing. Set the rest of the deck aside. Shuffle the cards and deal four cards to each child.

The players look at their cards to see if anyone has four-of-a-kind. If no one does, each player passes one card facedown to the player on his left. This continues until someone gets four-of-a-kind. The player who does get four-of-a-kind quietly puts his finger on the side of his nose. The other players then must put their fingers on the sides of their noses. The last one to touch his nose gets a strike. Three strikes and you are out. The trick is to watch the cards and watch the other players at the same time, especially after more and more cards have been passed.

Thirty-Six

This is a simple dice game that aids in developing counting and adding skills. The object of the game is to get as close as possible to thirty-six points without going over. The players each roll one die one time, with the highest number going first. That child rolls one die as many times as he or she wishes, adding up the points on each roll. If the total goes over thirty-six, the child is out of the game. Each child may stop at any time, at any total below thirty-six points, and pass to the next player.

Threes

This game requires three dice, and a pencil and paper to keep score. The children go in turn, and there is no advantage to going first.

The first child throws all three dice and puts aside the die with the highest number. That child then rolls the other two dice, and again puts aside the die with the highest number. The child then rolls the last die again, and his or her score is the total of the three dice. If the player rolls a triple on the first throw, only one of the dice is set aside, and the other two are rolled again. If the player rolls a double on the first throw, if the double number is higher than the third die, one of the double dice is put aside and two are thrown again. If the third die is higher than the double, then it is set aside and the other two dice are rolled again. If a player throws a double on the second turn, those two dice are counted in his or her score and the player does not make a third roll.

Play continues for a given number of rounds, say five or ten times around. The player with the highest total at the end of the rounds is the winner.

War

War is a two-player game, good for small children because it involves no card skills or decisions. For a group, have a tournament or split into teams and have simultaneous games, with members of one team paired against members of the other.

Shuffle the cards and deal the entire deck between the two players. Players do not look at their cards, but keep them in a stack in front of them, facedown. The two players take the top cards from their stacks and turn them faceup. The player with the higher value (Ace high) wins the round, and takes both cards and puts them at the bottom of his or her stack.

If the two cards turned up are of the same value, a "war" takes place. Each child takes the next three cards off his or her stack and places them facedown in the center. The fourth card is then turned up. The player with the highest card here wins all the cards on the table. If the fourth cards match, the process is repeated.

The game continues until one child has all the cards. As an alternative, set a time limit, and the child with the most cards at the end of the time limit is the winner.

Party Activities

Painting

Have enough poster board, poster paints, and brushes to go around. Have all the children paint a picture of the same object (a doll, a toy, etc.), or just let their imaginations go wild. Have a good supply of old men's shirts on hand for smocks.

Sculpture

Have enough modeling clay to go around and turn the children loose. At the end of the session, bake the results according to the directions on the modeling clay package, and let the children take their work home.

Or, have a huge collection of old hardware, pieces of wood, scraps of cloth, etc., for the children to combine in various forms. Use glue or play dough to stick the pieces together.

Wrapping Paper

Wrapping paper can be taken home and given to parents, or used to wrap a present for the next big event. Use a potato stamp (see page 78) to print a pattern on wrapping paper. Make stippled wrapping paper by coating a sheet of glossy paper with poster paint. When the paint is almost dry, create a stipple effect by patting the paper lightly with a sponge.

For rippled paper, paint one side of a sheet of glossy paper with poster paint. Lay the paper, paint side down, on a piece of waxed paper. Press the paper down firmly, and then pull it up quickly.

Stencils

Stencils can be used to create wrapping paper, greeting cards, or household decoration. Have friends save waxed butter cartons for the stencils. Open the carton up and lay it flat on a block of scrap wood. Draw a design, using an appropriate solid object such as a cookie cutter or anything else that would be recognizable in outline. Cut out the design using an X-Acto knife. Put the stencil on a sheet of paper, dip a brush (preferably one designed for stencils) in poster paint, and brush the paint on the paper, applying from the edges of the cutout to the center.

T-Shirt Design

Have an inexpensive, plain white T-shirt for each guest to personally decorate. Decoration can be done with crayons, felt-tip markers, or iron-on patches. Shirts can also be finger-painted with fabric paint. These activities are best done out on the patio or in the garage.

Mr. Vegetable Head

A homemade version of the commercial Mr. Potato Head game is easy to do. Use vegetables such as turnips, potatoes, squash, etc., for the head. Features can be made from buttons, pins, scraps of cloth, or anything else that comes to mind.

Mr. Peanut Head

Any number of people or creatures can be fashioned from peanuts in the shell and pipe cleaners. Use the pipe cleaners for arms and legs, and to connect several peanuts together.

Beanbags

Let each child make a beanbag out of the toe of an old sock and a handful of dried beans or corn. Sew the bags closed for them, and let them decorate them with crayons, markers, or glued-on scraps of cloth. Follow that with a game of beanbag toss.

Balloon Decorating

Give each child a blown-up balloon and provide tempera paint, brushes, glue, buttons, scraps of cloth, ribbon, colored paper, or anything else you can think of. There is no winner, and each child takes home his or her creation.

Finger Paints

You can buy finger paints, or you can make your own at home. Make up the paints the day before, as they take some time to cool down. In a large pot, mix 2 cups of cold water, ½ cup of laundry starch, and ½ cup of soap flakes (not laundry detergent). Cook for a few minutes, stirring constantly, until the mixture becomes clear. Add 1 tablespoon of glycerin (available from the drugstore) and pour into several glass jars. Stir in food coloring in each jar as desired. Store homemade finger paints in the refrigerator. The glycerin acts as a preservative, but the paints will spoil relatively quickly.

Finger painting is best done in the garage. The second choice is on an old table set on a drop cloth or tarp in a room without carpeting. All involved should wear old clothes. (Guests should bring a change of clothes, or be provided with an old man's shirt to serve as a painting smock.) Give each child a large sheet of glossy shelf paper and turn him loose.

Soap Carving

The first choice for a location is outside. The second choice is a room without carpeting. Give each child a bar of soft, white soap, and as dull a knife as possible. Also give safety lessons before beginning.

Puppets

Finger puppets can be made by cutting the fingers off of old (or inexpensive new) gloves. Hand puppets can be made from socks (white socks work best). Have plenty of crayons, markers, glue, scraps of cloth, etc., for decorating.

Play Dough

For homemade play dough, mix 1 cup of white flour with ½ cup of salt and 2 tablespoons of oil. Add some food coloring to water, and mix in the water a little at a time until the mixture is the right consistency. Store in resealable plastic bags to keep from drying out.

Edible Play Dough

Children can sculpt creations out of edible play dough, and then eat their masterpieces at the end of the session. The needed ingredients are:

2 cups flour
4 cups oatmeal
1 cup water
1 cup white corn syrup
1 cup peanut butter
1 ¼ cup nonfat powdered milk
1 ¼ cup sifted confectioners' sugar

Combine the flour and oatmeal in a blender for 30 seconds. Add the water and knead well. Add the remaining ingredients and knead well. Add more flour if the mixture is too sticky to knead properly. Use peanuts, candy, sunflower seeds, chocolate chips, etc., for decorations.

Hand-Decorated Handkerchiefs

Give each child a plain white, inexpensive handkerchief. Have a large assortment of crayons on hand. Have the children decorate the handkerchiefs with the crayons, pressing hard to get the wax into the cloth. To fix the colors, place each finished handkerchief between two damp clothes and press with a warm iron.

Make a Clock

This is a combination of crafts and games, designed to keep small children happy and busy (and quiet). Ahead of time, prepare a cardboard clock face and a set of small cardboard squares with the numbers "1" through "12" on them for each child. Have the children sit in a circle and give each a clock face. Place all the numbers in a large pot and pass it around, having each child take twelve numbers from the pot without looking. The children then paste as many numbers as they can on their clocks. Each child then tosses his or her duplicate numbers back into the pot, and the pot is passed around again, with each child taking as many numbers as he still needs for his clock. The first child to get all twelve numbers is the winner, but all the children get to complete their clocks.

Potato Stamps

Cut large potatoes in half and give a half to each child. Have the children draw simple designs (an initial, a star, a circle, etc.) on the cut end of the potato half. Help the children cut away the background around the design, removing about ¼ inch of potato. Press the design end of the potato on a rubber stamp pad, and then on a sheet of paper.

Singing

Many children's songs are easy to learn and also involve some sort of motion or activity. The best songs are very repetitive, or change slightly from verse to verse, so that they are easily and quickly picked up by the children.

Song pages for some of the most popular of these follow:

"The Farmer in the Dell"

Have the children stand in a circle, with one child starting out as the farmer. Have the farmer pull one more child into the center to represent each "takes" verse. Then a child leaves the center for each "leaves" verse, until the "cheese stands alone."

> The farmer in the dell,
> The farmer in the dell,

Heigh-ho the derry-o,
The farmer in the dell.

The farmer takes a wife,
The farmer takes a wife,
Heigh-ho the derry-o,
The farmer takes a wife.

The wife takes a child . . .

The child takes a nurse . . .

The nurse takes a dog . . .

The dog takes a cat . . .

The cat takes a mouse . . .

The mouse takes the cheese . . .

The farmer leaves the dell . . .

The wife leaves the dell . . . etc.

The cheese stands alone . . .

"The Mulberry Bush"

The children hold hands and skip in a circle while singing the chorus, stopping to act out the words in the verse.

Here we go 'round the mulberry bush,
The mulberry bush,
The mulberry bush.
Here we go 'round the mulberry bush
So early in the morning.

This is the way we wash our clothes,
Wash our clothes,
Wash our clothes.
This is the way we wash our clothes
So early Monday morning.

This is the way we iron our clothes
So early Tuesday morning.

This is the way we mend our clothes
So early Wednesday morning.

This is the way we sweep our house
So early Thursday morning.

This is the way we scrub our floor
So early Friday morning.

This is the way we bake our bread
So early Saturday morning.

This is the way we stay in bed
So early Sunday morning.

"Ring Around the Rosie"

Have the children hold hands in a circle. Skip around in a circle while singing, and fall down at the end.

Ring around the Rosie,
A pocket full of posie,
Ashes, ashes,
All fall down.

"London Bridge"

This is another traditional combination of game and song. As the song is sung, two of the children join hands and hold them high in the air to allow the other children to march under the "bridge" in an endless circle. When the line "my fair lady" is sung, the bridge is dropped and the child passing under at the time is caught. This child replaces one of the two forming the bridge.

> London Bridge is falling down,
> falling down, falling down,
> London Bridge is falling down,
> My fair lady.
>
> Build it up with wood and clay,
> Wood and clay, wood and clay,
> Build it up with wood and clay,
> My fair lady.
>
> Wood and clay will wash away,
> Wash away, wash away,
> Wood and clay will wash away,
> My fair lady.
>
> Build it up with bricks and mortar,
> Bricks and mortar, bricks and mortar,
> Build it up with bricks and mortar,
> My fair lady.
>
> Bricks and mortar will not stay,
> Will not stay, will not stay,
> Bricks and mortar will not stay,
> My fair lady.

Build it up with iron and steel,
Iron and steel, iron and steel,
Build it up with iron and steel,
My fair lady.

Iron and steel will bend and bow,
Bend and bow, bend and bow,
Iron and steel will bend and bow,
My fair lady.

Build it up with silver and gold,
Silver and gold, silver and gold,
Build it up with silver and gold,
My fair lady.

Silver and gold are stolen away,
Stolen away, stolen away,
Silver and gold are stolen away,
My fair lady.

Set a man to watch all night,
Watch all night, watch all night,
Set a man to watch all night,
My fair lady.

"Inky Dinky Spider"

Teach the children to act out the various parts of the song. Flexed or wiggled fingers simulate a spider climbing up the spout at the beginning and end of the song. Arms stretched overhead, and then brought down with fluttering fingers, acts out rain. Arms in a circle over the head, with fingertips touching, symbolize the sun.

Inky dinky spider
Went up the water spout.
Down came the rain
And washed the spider out.
Out came the sun and dried up all the rain.
And the inky dinky spider
Climbed up the spout again.

Check your local bookstore for additional books with songs and musical games, as well as for records and tapes. Check the music store for children's sing-along albums, and also check the video store for similar material.

Party Food
and Refreshments

Birthday parties means cake and ice cream. Anything
beyond that is a bonus as far as kids are concerned.

Therefore, put most of your effort into the cake. Decorated birthday cakes can be purchased at most bakeries and
major grocery stores.

If you have the time and inclination, you can make your
own for less money, and can create a cake which uniquely
matches the tastes of your child (chocolate cake with peanut
butter icing?), or perfectly matches the theme of the party.

An easy way to do your own cake is to use cake mix
and ready-made frostings to build the basics, then knock
yourself out with the decorations.

If you want to do it totally from scratch, there is cake-
making and cake-decorating advice later in this chapter,
and recipes for cakes and icings are in Chapter 8.

Party refreshments should be geared to the age group of
the party guests.

But you should also keep in mind that for kids, as long
as the food is tasty and plentiful, you don't need to go

overboard with gourmet treats. In fact, you can keep the menu very simple—hot dogs or pizza, chips, and cake—and be sure of pleasing most kids.

This is not to say you shouldn't put in the extra effort if that is what you enjoy doing. If you like to experiment in the kitchen, go ahead, but once again, keep in mind the age and tastes of the guests. Blue-cheese olive balls probably won't play great at any kids' party.

If you find yourself hosting a party for older children or teenagers, and you aren't familiar with their eating habits, ask around. They can be picky, and they can eat a lot more than you might imagine! Especially for teens, have more than you think you'll need.

Generally, for kids parties, you can time them so you don't need to serve a meal. Snacks are plenty.

A birthday cake, however, is essential. So go all out on the cake!

Planning

Keep the age group in mind when planning the amount of food to buy and prepare. Smaller kids have small appetites to start with, and may get too wound up in the party activities to eat very much. Big kids will have bigger appetites, and if you are planning a party for teenagers, buy big!

Also keep the age group in mind when deciding on the types of food to be served. For younger kids, keep the danger of choking in mind, and avoid small hard items such as hard candies or peanuts. Kids will be excited and trying to eat, talk, and play all at the same time. Have plenty of supervision during food service, to keep the kids seated and as quiet as possible while they're eating.

If you are making the food in advance, or serving it outdoors during warm weather, keep food safety in mind. Make sure the food preparation area is clean, and that food is properly stored between advance preparation and the actual serving time.

Shopping

Plan to do all your shopping at least a day or two before the party. This will give you time to figure out whether you've forgotten anything, and it will avoid a last-minute rush.

As you are planning the party, keep a running list of everything you need, and then do all your shopping at the same time to avoid a lot of extra running around.

Make a copy of the shopping list below to make sure you get all the essentials needed for the party.

Shopping List
Misc. Items
Invitations
Postage stamps
Decorations:
    balloons
    crepe paper
    other:
Favors
Prizes for games
Game/activity materials
Film/videotape/batteries
Trash bags, cleaning supplies
Food Service
Tablecloth

Plates
Bowls
Spoons and forks
Cake
Cake ordered or
Cake ingredients:
  baking powder
  baking soda
  butter/shortening
  chocolate/cocoa
  eggs
  flour
  milk
  sugar
  vanilla
  other:
Cake Decorations
Candles
Assorted decorations
Frosting or
Frosting ingredients:
  butter
  confectioners' sugar
  milk
  vanilla
  other flavorings, ingredients:
Other foods
Main meal items
Punch/beverages
Snacks

Serving Tips

Definitely consider using disposable tableware for the party, especially if there are more than several guests. For this one day a year, you might at least think about suspending your environmental concerns—you will have enough cleanup to worry about without adding a huge load of dirty dishes.

If you just won't use disposables, be sure you have enough unbreakable glasses, plates, bowls and tableware to serve everyone. Also be sure you have a tablecloth or placemats and napkins which will stand up to the potential abuse.

Don't try to have a buffet for younger kids. Get them seated and serve them.

If the party is for infants or toddlers, make it clear that the accompanying parent is responsible for getting the guest fed. Have some appropriate snacks and beverages available for the parents, ideally something they can eat with one hand while holding onto a child.

Participation by Kids

When kids are old enough, it can be fun to have them participate in preparing the food. Some theme parties, such as a Restaurant theme, particularly lend themselves to this approach. The preparation of the food, such as making pizza, becomes one of the main party activities.

Another enjoyable way to get kids involved, and to have them express their creativity, is for them to decorate the cake, or decorate cupcakes to take home as party favors.

Naturally, when kids are involved in the food preparation process, they should be warned in advance so they can dress appropriately, or you should provide adequate protection, such as aprons or smocks.

Extra adult supervision might also be required for an activity of this sort. Be especially aware and careful of sharp or hot objects.

Foods to Fit Theme Parties

Fitting the food to a theme party is really a lot easier than it might seem. It is mainly an exercise in gentle deception. You just take whatever it is you really want to serve, then give it an appropriate name and serve it in the appropriate manner.

Who could argue that any punch served in a "tankard" and called "Pirate's Punch" was not indeed pirate's punch?

Party food should be fun food, so let yourself loose. Look at everything in your kitchen from a new perspective—cookie cutters aren't just for cookies! Use cookie cutters on sandwiches, cheese slices, fruit slices, brownies, or thin sheets of Rice Krispies Treats.

Certainly you can come up with some more imaginative ways to use food coloring and cake decorating kits.

Travel up and down the aisles of the grocery store with the same outlook. Don't limit yourself to the usual grocery aisles, either. Explore some nooks of the local supermarket that you don't generally visit.

Check the housewares aisle, or health and beauty. You might come up with just the right idea for odd but perfect cake decorations.

Just use your imagination to fit the food to the party. Chapter 6 lists a number of theme ideas, and some food ideas for each.

Tips & Hints

Cake Making Hints

If you are making a layer cake, keep the two cake pans at least two inches apart in the oven. If they are too close together, they layers may bake unevenly.

Use fresh baking powder to insure that your cake rises properly. If you aren't sure if your baking powder is still good, test it by putting ½ teaspoon of it into ¼ cup of hot water. The powder is still good if it bubbles.

If your brown sugar has gotten too hard to use, put it in an airtight jar with a wedge of fresh apple. It will soften up enough to use in about a day. To soften it immediately, put it in the microwave for just a few seconds, repeat until soft, but be careful not to get it too hot or it will melt!

Use unsalted butter. If you use salted butter or margarine, reduce the added salt by ¾ teaspoon per half-pound of butter.

Testing for doneness: The cake should be browned and pulling away from the edges of the pan. A cake tester or toothpick inserted into the middle should come out clean.

Cooling: When the cake is done, place it on a cooling rack in the pan for about five minutes, then turn it out onto the rack to cool completely. To cool a cake in a hurry, pop it in the freezer while you make the frosting. By the time the frosting is ready, the cake should be cool enough to pop out of the pan.

Cake Pans: Cake batter should only fill the pan about halfway (never over two-thirds) to allow the cake to rise. If you don't have the size pan called for in a recipe, choose a pan or combination of pans which have about the same number of square inches from the chart below. If you fill the pan and have batter left over, make another small cake or some cupcakes with it.

Pan size	Square Inches
8″ x 1 ½″ round	50
8″ x 8″ x 1 ½″	64
9″ x 1 ½″ round	64
9″ x 9″ x 1 ½″	81
10″ x 1 ½″ round	79
11″ x 7″ x 1 ½″	77
13″ x 9″ x 2″	117
15″ x 10″ x 2″	150

Cake Decorating

Cakes should be frosted as soon as they are barely cool. This will keep them moist.

Use your imagination in finding materials to make cake decorations. Many foods can be crafted into decorations. Check out the supermarket aisles for ideas, and browse through some books on cake decorating. Generally, parenting and family magazines will have at least one big party special each year with specific ideas and decorating instructions.

When you are going to draw a design on a cake with frosting, first trace the design into the base frosting using a toothpick or other fine-pointed tool, then go over the outline with the frosting. Another easy way to outline designs is to use cookie cutters to make an impression on the cake, then outline it with frosting.

Put the cake on the serving platter prior to frosting it. Slide pieces of waxed paper under the cake all around before frosting; then, when you're done, pull out the waxed paper and you have a frosted cake on a clean serving platter.

Make a batch of Decorating Icing (recipe in Chapter 8) and divide it into smaller portions to color with food coloring if necessary. Use a pastry bag to apply the icing. Ready-made colored icings in tubes are available at most supermarkets.

Some of the foods which are easily pressed into service as decorations include:

- Licorice strings (rope, laces, whiskers)
- Marshmallows (snowballs, rocks)
- Fruit leather (can be formed into cones, cut into shapes)
- Cookies (can be cut or formed into shapes for wheels, stars, logs, and more)
- Jelly beans (eyes)
- Gumdrops (funny noses, or cut up to make other shapes)

Costumes

Kids love to play "pretend" and to dress up in costumes. This makes a costume party, or even a costume game, a natural for a children's party. It goes without saying that costumes are a must for Halloween parties.

A prime rule to remember here is that the costume must work for the child. Don't force the child into your own elaborate scheme if he or she only wants an inexpensive dime-store mask of a favorite cartoon character.

Two major considerations in buying or making a costume are safety and comfort.

Safety: Be sure the child can move freely, that major costume elements are not highly flammable, and that there are not parts hanging from the costume which can become tangled and choke or trap a child.

Comfort: A major complaint children might have about any costume is that it's uncomfortable—too tight or, more often, itchy. (This applies as well to that most objectionable of all costumes, the suit and tie on a little boy!) A child wearing a tight, itchy costume certainly will not be able to enjoy a party.

Comfort takes on a different concern for outdoor activities, such as trick-or-treating: whether the costume will keep the child warm and dry.

Quick Costume Tip

For an instant, all-purpose costume base, use a sweatshirt and sweat pants (or for summer, a T-shirt and leggings or bicycle pants).

This basic outfit can be painted, have things sewn onto it, glued onto it, or hung off of it.

It is comfortable, inexpensive, and it is not critical if it gets damaged or soiled.

Costume Chest

Families with young children should have a "Costume Chest" on hand. Not only is such a chest (or box or suitcase) a great source of instant costumes when needed for parties, it can also be called upon to provide a diverting rainy-day activity.

The Costume Chest need not be an expensive undertaking. As opposed to running out at the last minute to buy an expensive ready-made costume, the Costume Chest can be added to all year with finds from garage sales, thrift stores, and bargain tables. Even less expensive sources for Costume Chest items are relatives' basements, attics, and closets. Grandma and Grandpa are always good sources for unique items sure to fascinate contemporary kids.

Good Costume Box staples include:

- "Magic wands"
- "Royal scepters"
- "Swords"
- Bandannas
- Boots
- Canes, umbrellas, walking sticks
- Cheerleader batons

- Coats
- Costume jewelry
- Face paints
- Fake furs
- Gloves
- Hats
  baseball caps
  crowns
  firefighter helmets
  football helmets
  hard hats
  military hats
  police hats
  western hats
- Neckties
- Old Halloween masks
  and costumes
- Old towels, sheets,
  blankets (to make tents,
  capes, robes)
- Scarves
- Shoes
- Sport uniforms
- Unusual fabric remnants

Party Theme Costumes

If you decide to have a costume theme party, there will be obvious costume choices. Following, in Chapter 6, are some tips and ideas for costumes appropriate for various theme parties.

Making Costumes

If you want to make an elaborate costume for a child for a very special party, or for Halloween, check the library for costume books, or check with a sewing store for patterns.

Also check the September and October issues of various magazines aimed at families and parents. These will often have ideas and instructions for making costumes.

(A good book with plenty of ideas and instructions is *Jane Asher's Costume Book*, Open Chain Publishing.)

For quickly putting together simple, fun costumes, pull together a simple collection of materials and tools, including the following and others you can think of. With this collection of materials and tools, combined with one or more active imaginations, you should be able to assemble a wide variety of costumes, from angels, to robots, to monsters.

A fun party game might be to provide these items and challenge the guests to come up with costumes. It's amazing how few items you need to make an amazing costume—with only a roll or two of toilet paper and some cellophane tape, you can be a mummy!

Materials and Tools

- aluminum foil
- assorted notions (pins, buttons, etc.)
- balloons
- black heavy marker
- bubble wrap
- burlap
- buttons
- cardboard tubes
- cardboard boxes, assorted sizes
- clear plastic
- colored markers
- contact paper
- cotton balls
- crayons
- crepe paper
- egg cartons
- elastic
- eyelets
- fabric remnants
- feathers
- felt
- glitter
- glue
- gummed stars
- hole punch
- hot glue gun
- needles and thread
- old sheets and towels
- paintbrushes
- paints (poster and watercolors)
- paper bags
- paper towels
- pencils
- pens
- pie tins
- pipe cleaners
- plastic foam
- pliers (for bending wire)
- poster board
- ribbon, assorted
- rivet gun and rivets
- rubber bands
- ruler

- safety pins
- scissors
- sequins
- socks
- spring clip clothespins
- stapler and staples
- straight pins
- string
- T-shirts
- tape, assorted
  (cellophane, duct, electrical)
- tape measure
- toilet paper
- twine
- Velcro
- wire
- wire cutter
- wood scraps

Theme and Holiday Parties

A birthday party with a theme seems more like an event for children. The food, decor, activities, and even costumes can be coordinated to make the day as much fun as a trip to an amusement park. And unless you are planning a surprise party, the guest of honor can get several days of enjoyment from helping plan and prepare for the party.

Theme parties do not have to be any more complicated or difficult than any other kind of party. Simply pick some topic or activity that is fun for your birthday child (whatever he or she currently spends every waking hour doing or talking about or asking for) and plan appropriate tie-ins between the theme and the basic elements of a birthday party: food and games.

Birthday Themes

There are suggestions given for each theme below. Let these ideas get you started thinking about other things to do. Change and expand on these suggestions, and come up with ideas of your own. You can even come up with whole new themes of your own, based on what your child likes to do. Once you have decided on a theme, glance through the other theme suggestions listed here and read through the games and activities sections of this book for other ideas which you can adapt to your theme.

Unless the party is planned as a surprise, you can sit down with the guest of honor and some of his or her friends and brain-storm a theme party. Having the children bounce ideas off of one another, with an adult present to keep the party budget smaller than the household budget, is one of the best ways to develop some very creative party ideas.

Academy Awards Party

The glamour of Hollywood and the fun of favorite movies combine in an Academy Awards party. This can be near the time of the actual awards, or just any time of year.

Invitations: Cut out the invitation in the shape of an Oscar, or make it resemble an award envelope with a wax seal and ribbon. Another choice is to make the invitation look like a movie ticket.

Decorations: A large cut-out of the award, movie posters, stars with the guests' names on them.

Favors/Prizes: Movie posters, movie magazines, movie passes, videotapes of movies, bags of popcorn, theater-style boxes of candy.

Games/Activities: Try a trivia game with questions from some of the guests' favorite movies. Be sure that most of the guests have seen the movie, or that they are movies that everyone in that age group is familiar with.

Food: Popcorn, candy, other items served "theater style" from a "concession stand." Another option is to have a glamorous awards "reception" for the food.

Costumes: Have everyone dress very "Hollywood," playing dress-up, with plenty of jewelry and sunglasses; or, have them dress as a favorite movie character.

Airplane Party

Invitations: Write your invitations with a heavy black marker on photocopies of an airline schedule, or on actual schedules if you can get enough copies. Or send balsa glider kits as the invitations, with directions to the party included.

Decorations: Travel posters and pictures or posters of airplanes will liven up the walls.

Favors/Prizes: Check with an airline ticket office for the wings that flight attendants hand out to children on the airlines. Toy or hobby stores should have inexpensive planes that actually fly, either balsa wood gliders or light-weight models with rubber-band, wind-up propellers. For older children, plastic airplane models can be given as game prizes.

Games/Activities: Give each child a balsa wood or polystyrene glider and have races, distance contests, or relays.

Rent a movie featuring airplanes. Depending on the ages and interests of the guests, you might want to get a documentary about flying, a war movie featuring air combat, or one of the *Airport* films.

Food: If the children are old enough to know about flying on commercial airplanes, some sort of takeoff on airline food can be fun. Serve child-edition frozen dinners, or a box lunch with a sandwich, a candy bar, and a small apple. Serve the food from a tea cart or a TV stand with wheels.

Costumes: Flying costumes can be done without a lot of expense with a little imagination. A pilot's uniform can be approximated with blue dress pants, a white shirt and dark tie, and a pair of wings pinned on over the shirt pocket. Dress your kitchen helpers as flight attendants, with dark blue pants, a white or striped shirt, and a dark blue apron.

Alphabet Party

An alphabet party is a natural for *Sesame Street* fans. Check out *Sesame Street* books and shows for more ideas, and rent *Sesame Street* videos to help keep the children amused.

Invitations: Make the invitations by using large cut-out letters from newspapers or magazines for the first letter of each sentence or paragraph.

Decorations: Decorate the house with large cut-out letters of different styles and sizes, with posters featuring typography or graphics, and with pictures of things or animals, each with a large cut-out of its initial pasted on it.

Favors/Prizes: Coloring books or readers based on the alphabet are good for preschoolers, as are alphabet blocks.

Games/Activities: Activities can include words games, such as finding as many words as possible made up of the letters in "Happy Birthday," a spelling bee, or cutting out letters and making posters with family names.

For small children, give each a cut-out letter and have him place it on a picture or an item of furniture that starts with that letter. This could be a team event, with each team given a stack of letters.

Have the children draw slips of paper out of an envelope, each with a letter on it. Then have them draw, or paint, or sculpt something that starts with that letter.

Food: Alphabet soup, of course, is a natural. (You might want to stretch things and serve such dishes as "p" soup or iced "t.") Sandwiches can be trimmed in the shape of letters, each in the initial of a guest. Paint each guest's initial on a sandwich with food coloring and a small brush.

Costumes: Send out advance notice, and challenge the children's creativity in dressing with an alphabet theme. Have the children wear as many items as possible starting with the same letter (cap and cape, pants and parka, etc.), or have each wear something that starts with one of their initials.

Archaeology Party

Invitations: Photocopy an old map, drawing lines, notes, and an "X" or two on it to make it look like a treasure map, and write your invitations on copies.

Decorations: Look for travel posters or airline posters of Egyptian pyramids, Incan temple ruins, and southwestern American cliff dwellings.

Favors/Prizes: For small children, sand pails and shovels to keep after a "dig" in the sand box for treasures.

Games/Activities: A hunt for buried treasure is a natural. You probably don't want a horde of children actually digging up your yard, so "bury" the treasure under leaves, in a sandbox, behind trees, under gardening equipment, and so on.

Finish up with a showing of one of the Indiana Jones movies.

Food: Serve box lunches in the yard as a break from digging for treasures.

Costumes: Work shirts, khaki shorts, and boots or old shoes approximate work clothes for an archaeological dig.

Artist Party

Invitations: These can be handmade, or use postcards with illustrations of famous works of art. These should be available at an art supply store, a large book store, a college or university, or your local art museum. If you can't find ready-made cards, make your own with illustrations cut from art magazines, usually readily available at a good-sized newsstand or bookstore.

Favors/Prizes: Depending on the age group, colored pencils, colored markers, crayons and coloring books, commercial or homemade play dough, or boxes of modeling clay all make good giveaways.

Games/Activities: Activities during the party can include drawing, tracing, sculpting with modeling clay or Play-Doh, T-shirt painting, etc. See the "Games and Activities" chapter of this book for more details on artist activities.

Food: The refreshments can be served as if at a gallery opening. Place the art created by the children on display around the room. Serve lemon-lime soda in disposable plastic champagne glasses and put out platters of cheese and sausage cubes on toothpicks. The birthday cake can be a pan cake cut in the shape of an artist's palette. Partially freeze the cake to make it easier to cut to shape, cover the whole cake with white frosting, and then apply daubs of various colored frosting for the paints.

Costumes: For simple costumes, have some old men's dress shirts for smocks and let the children daub and smear them with finger paints as a first game. (This is best done outside, in a garage, or in an unfinished basement.)

Astrology Party

Invitations: Customize each guest's invitation with a copy of his or her latest horoscope. Or make up a horoscope for the guest of honor, and include the invitation in the horoscope, using the same style of writing.

Decorations: Decorate the walls with astrological posters, or pictures or posters showing space, the planets, or stars.

Favors/Prizes: Have each child's horoscope printed out

by a computer, or buy inexpensive horoscope books.

Games/Activities: Have a fortune-teller or card reader do a reading for each child. (A friend, unknown to the children, can be briefed with a few facts about each, and give palm readings.)

Food: Decorate cookies or a cake with signs of the zodiac drawn with icing.

Costumes: For the first activity, have the children draw their own signs of the zodiac and wear them as badges for the rest of the party.

Astronomy Party

Invitations: Write your invitations on postcards with scenes of outer space on them.

Decorations: Get posters of space scenes, rockets, or outer space movies. Hang rocket ship models from the ceiling.

Favors/Prizes: Depending on the age of the guests, give outer space coloring books, ray guns, toy rockets, plastic rocket models, or books about the stars.

Games/Activities: Set up a treasure hunt with a space theme and space-related prizes.

Wind up the party with one of the *Star Wars* movies.

Food: Serve orange drink in water bottles with straws. Pack trail mix in zip-lock plastic bags for snacks. Reusable plastic food tubes are available from sporting goods stores with extensive camping departments. Fill with pudding or yogurt.

Costumes: Matching colored T-shirts with military-like emblems can serve as spaceship uniforms.

Automobile Party

Invitations: Make your own invitations, decorating them with pictures cut out of automotive magazines. Or make photocopies of a street map and write the invitation over the map with a heavy black marker.

Decorations: Hang posters or large pictures of cars on the walls and place automotive magazines around the room. Stop in at a few new car dealerships and pick up some brochures to place around.

Favors/Prizes: Depending on the ages and interests of the guests, you can buy automotive magazines, car posters, small toy cars, or plastic models of current, classic, or race cars.

Games/Activities: Set up an automobile scavenger hunt, giving each team a list of various cars and trucks they must spot and check off. For older children, make a list of scrambled automobile names and have them sort them out, individually or in teams. (FROD = FORD, AINNSS = NISSAN, etc.)

Finish up with a documentary video about cars, or a classic movie about car racing, such as *Le Mans*.

Food: Serve drive-in food, on trays if possible. A good menu would be hamburgers wrapped in waxed paper, fries (check the supermarket for frozen fries in individual-serving boxes), and root beer in mugs.

Costumes: Anything suggesting driving works well, including leather gloves, sun glasses, scarves, hats, and light jackets.

Backward Party

Invitations: Start with invitations printed backward, so that they can be read while held up to the mirror. Instruct the children that all outer clothing must be put on backward.

Decorations: "Happy Birthday" signs should be printed backward, and any other decorations should be hung backward or upside-down. Turn chairs so that they face the wall or have their backs to the table. If possible, turn paintings to the wall. Greet the arriving guests by saying "Good-bye," and have them walk backward into the house.

Games/Activities: Plan activities that involve some hand coordination, whether relay races (walking backward) with spoons of water, drawing, coloring, etc., and have the right-handed children use their left hands, and vice versa.

Play word games, such as having each child write down (backward) as many words as possible using the letters in "yadhtriB yppaH."

Food: The menu should start with dessert, and work backward to a main course. The cake can be served upside-down, with the frosting on the bottom. Follow this with sandwiches and then with a salad or appetizers, such as nuts, or chips and dips.

Costumes: Any clothing worn backward works fine for this party.

Band Party

Invitations: Write the invitations with a large black marker on old sheets of music.

Decorations: Hang posters, or pictures of musicians or rock bands on the walls.

Favors/Prizes: Have an assortment of toy instruments (drums, penny whistles, etc.) to give out and to work into various games.

Games/Activities: The children can play along in such song games as "Farmer in the Dell" or "London Bridge," or in "Musical Chairs" or "Drop the Hanky."

Another good game to play is "Orchestra," as described in the "Games and Activities" chapter of this book.

Food: Serve typical rock-concert refreshments, including hot dogs, popcorn, peanuts, and ice-cream.

Costumes: Guests can dress up as their favorite rock

musicians, uniformed band members, or classical musicians.

Baseball Party

Invitations: Make the invitations with pictures cut out of the sports section of the newspaper, or from a baseball magazine. An alternative is to use baseball trading cards, writing the invitation on the back of a card, or taping a typed invitation to a package of cards.

Decorations: Hang posters of major league baseball stars on the walls. Flags and red, white, and blue bunting or streamers also contribute to the atmosphere. If possible, get some pennants of some major league teams.

Favors/Prizes: For party favors, have baseball caps, with each child's name lettered on the front. Prizes for game winners can include baseballs, bats, trading cards, and other related items.

Games/Activities: Activities can include going to a baseball game (if the group is small enough) or playing a baseball game (if the group is large enough). If you are going to have your own ball game, use a nearby large field or a park. As an alternative, play baseball using a broomstick and a small rubber ball, using a beach ball and a broom for a bat, or using a balloon for the ball and an open hand for a bat.

To wind down the party, rent a classic baseball movie, such as *The Babe Ruth Story*.

Food: Refreshments, of course, include peanuts in the shell (not in the house), Cracker Jacks, hot dogs, and sodas in paper cups.

Costumes: Have the guests wear any baseball-related clothing that they might have, including caps, T-shirts, or team jackets.

Beach Party

Invitations: Use postcards with beach scenes for invitations, or make your own invitations with pictures cut out of travel magazines. Put a few grains of sand in each invitation envelope so that it will spill out when opened. (But not enough to make a real mess.)

Decorations: Decorate the walls with travel posters showing water, beaches, or surfing. Drape beach towels over chairs, or use them for table coverings.

Favors/Prizes: Get a plastic pail for each child, and write the name on the outside with a large black marker. Use the pail to serve a picnic lunch, and for games later, such as building sand castles.

Games/Activities: If you don't have the use of a swimming pool, buy or borrow several inexpensive plastic wading pools. Hoses, sprinklers, or other water toys add to the fun. If you don't have a sandbox, make a square of old boards and line it with a large tarp. You can buy sand at most large hardware stores or building suppliers. Get plenty of inexpensive beach toys, including beach balls.

The sandbox can be used for a treasure hunt, hiding coins or small prizes in the sand. Plan lots of outdoor, wet, messy games, such as water balloon tosses, water relay races, etc.

Rent an appropriate movie, such as one of the early Frankie Avalon beach party films, and show it to wind down the party.

Food: Serve any traditional picnic foods, including fried chicken, sandwiches, potato salad, and veggie sticks. Serve soft drinks in cans or lemonade from a large insulated jug.

Costumes: Swimsuits, beach shirts and shorts, and other casual clothes are all appropriate.

Bike Party

All of the children invited should have bikes and should ride them to the party.

Invitations: Make your own by writing with a black marker on photocopies of a map of a local bike trail, or custom decorate invitations with pictures cut out of a bicycling magazine.

Decorations: Most of the activity should take place outside, so you don't have to worry too much about decorating the house. Get some advertising posters from a bike shop, or travel posters highlighting bike tours.

Favors/Prizes: Many small and inexpensive bicycling items are available from bike shops or sporting goods stores. Possibilities include water bottles, cycling gloves, cycling hats, and T-shirts.

Games/Activities: Any number of games from the "Games and Activities" chapter of this book can be adapted to be played on bikes. These include relay races, treasure hunts, scavenger hunts, Simon Says, Mother May I, and Follow the Leader.

Bikes can be decorated for the day with streamers, balloons, and finger-paints. Races should be set up stressing skills rather than pure speed. Set up a race course with obstacles that keep speed down, and with tasks, such as breaking a balloon with the front tire, along the way.

Wind down the party with a rented video. Get a documentary on bicycle racing, or get *Breaking Away*, a modern classic about boys and bike racing.

Food: Refreshments can include healthy snacks favored by bicycle racers, such as bananas or granola bars. Water or other drinks can be served in water bottles which the children can keep as party favors.

Costumes: Cycling gear ranges from the casual to the

high tech. The children can wear anything from T-shirts and shorts to cycling shorts and jerseys with racing helmets.

Camping Party

Invitations: Write your invitations on photocopies of a map of a wilderness area or a brochure for a state or national park. Include a list of "camping gear" each child should bring to the party, like a flashlight, a sweater or jacket, and a plastic cup, preferably in a backpack.

Decorations: Have rustic-looking signs starting in the front yard to direct arriving children to the "camp grounds" in the rear of the house. You might want to rent a large caterer's tent for atmosphere, and in case of rain. If you have camping gear, you may want to use it as well as borrowing or renting some more.

Favors/Prizes: Check out the camping section of a large sporting goods store for small, inexpensive items such as compasses, pocket flashlights, and so on.

Games/Activities: You may want to have one or two special guests actually spend the night with the birthday child. They can camp out in a tent in the backyard, or in a tent made of sheets or blankets in a bedroom or family room. If the children are actually sleeping outside, make sure that they have adequate sleeping bags or other covers and a bug-proof tent.

Activities can include treasure hunts or scavenger hunts with an emphasis on natural items. Also, tag, "Hide-and-Seek," and relay races are good outdoor fun.

To cap off the party while settling down the children, show an appropriate rented video, such as a wildlife documentary.

Food: Keep the food simple; cook it over an open fire, or at least a camp stove or a barbecue grill. Hot dogs or hamburgers are good. The best thing to do, if possible, is to have each child cook his or her own hot dog on a stick over a fire or coals. This activity needs to be closely supervised with any age group, to avoid both burned hot dogs and burned children. Finish up with toasted marshmallows.

Costumes: Have the children dress up for "roughing it." Jeans, flannel shirts, hiking boots, and caps make up the basics. Add a down vest or a parka if the weather is chilly.

Cartoon Party

Invitations: Make the invitations out of comic strips from the Sunday paper. Paste pieces of white paper over the dialogue balloons in the comics, and write in your own dialogue, inviting the children to the party and giving the details.

Decorations: Hang copies of the Sunday comics on the walls, as well as posters for cartoon movies.

Favors/Prizes: Have a large selection of small plastic cartoon figures, enough to go around.

Games/Activities: Have the children decorate shoe boxes with cartoon characters, taking the boxes home for storing their valuable stuff.

Rent some videos with favorite cartoons (Road Runner, Bugs Bunny) and perhaps a full-length cartoon feature, such as *Roger Rabbit* or the *Ninja Turtles*.

Food: Serve "movie" refreshments during the cartoons, including soda (in paper cups, if possible) and lots of popcorn.

Costumes: Have each child come as his or her favorite comic strip or cartoon character.

Casino Party

This theme party is best for older children who can learn card and other games, and who have some grasp of the idea of gambling for money.

Invitations: Make your own by pasting the details of the party on old playing cards; or, larger invitations can be decorated with playing cards.

Decorations: Set up the room as a casino, including green cloth over the "gaming" tables.

Favors/Prizes: Party favors could include decks of cards or dice. One variation is to give each child a packet of play money at the start of the party, and let each child keep whatever he or she has at the end of the party.

Games/Activities: The best games are simple ones that everyone can play at once. If you can find a toy roulette wheel, this is a great game for keeping children interested. Simplify the rules, such as only having bets on red or black, odd or even, and single numbers.

You may also want to play a simplified game of craps. Mark off two areas on a table, one for bets that the "shooter" will win, the other for bets that the shooter will lose. After all bets are made, the shooter throws the dice. If seven or eleven come up, the shooter wins. If two, three, or twelve come up, the shooter loses. Any other number is then the shooter's "point." The shooter keeps rolling the dice until the point comes up, and the shooter wins, or a seven comes up, and the shooter loses.

Younger children can play other card games for play money. Many card games are described in the "Games and Activities" chapter of this book.

Food: Refreshments during the party can include juice in plastic disposable wine glasses and fancy looking snacks made of cold cuts and cheeses. The birthday cake can be decorated with cards and dice or with play money.

Costumes: Costumes can provide a subtheme to this party. Possibilities include riverboat gambler costumes, more formal attire (as for a European casino), or touristy styles (anything goes) à la Las Vegas.

Circus Party

Invitations: Make the invitations in the form of circus tickets, hand-drawn or copied on colored paper.

Decorations: The ultimate circus environment is the "Big Top." You can spare yourself the expense of renting a large tent by using a camping dining canopy. This is available at sporting goods stores and is relatively inexpensive. Or you can create a tent-like atmosphere in your house by decorating a large room. Run paper streamers from the center of the ceiling or a chandelier to points along the walls, making a tent-like canopy.

Favors/Prizes: Depending on the ages and interests of the children, small stuffed animals or plastic animal figures make good gifts.

Games/Activities: If the children don't wear costumes, have them paint their faces as clowns. Get theatrical makeup if available, or use regular makeup, such as lipstick and mascara. Have plenty of clean-up supplies on hand.

Make clown hats by forming and taping large sheets of heavy colored paper into cone shapes, decorating the hats with cotton balls, paper pom-poms, and pieces of other colored paper cut into various shapes.

Wind up the party with a circus movie, such as *The Greatest Show on Earth.*

Food: Set up a refreshment stand in a corner of the room or in the yard. Serve hot dogs wrapped in wax paper, sodas in large paper cups, peanuts and popcorn in bags, and ice-cream cones. Make ice-cream clowns by putting a scoop of ice cream on a saucer, putting an ice-cream cone on top as a clown hat, and making a face with candy and nuts.

Costumes: The children can come dressed up as clowns, acrobats, or other favorite circus performers.

Color Party

The idea of this party theme is to concentrate on colors in general, or on a particular color, such as the guest-of-honor's favorite color.

Invitations: Make the invitations as colorful as possible, and explain the concept and what the guests should do or bring. If each child is going to have a different theme color, assign one in the invitation, or have the children call and pick out a favorite color, making sure that they don't all pick the same one.

Decorations: Drape the room with colored streamers. Hang the walls with pictures and posters, all with the same dominant color.

Favors/Prizes: Coloring books and crayons are good gifts, and can be used to keep the children busy.

Games/Activities: Put together arts and crafts activities focusing on colors. For example, divide the children into teams and give each a list of scrambled letters that can be rearranged to spell out colors (nereg = green, greano = orange, etc.) Or decorate T-shirts with favorite colors (see the chapter on "Games and Activities" in this book.)

Food: Try to follow through on a color theme, such as serving several foods of the same color. Bake cookies or a cake, using food coloring to match the theme color.

Costumes: Have the children dress entirely in one color, either all of them in the same color, or each in his or her own color.

Comic Book Party

Invitations: Make invitations out of comic book pages, blanking out the dialogue balloons and writing in your own dialogue about the party.

Decorations: Get posters of comic book characters and movie posters of cartoons.

Favors/Prizes: Have a selection of comic books that are popular with your child's age group.

Games/Activities: Have the children draw or sculpt their favorite comic book characters.

Show an animated movie based on comic book characters, such as the Ninja Turtles.

Food: The ideal meal for comic books is pizza and soda.

Costumes: Have each child dress up as his or her favorite comic book character.

Dinosaur Party

Invitations: Trace outlines of dinosaurs on construction paper, cut them out, and write your invitations on them.

Decorations: Get posters or pictures of dinosaurs from a bookstore or a natural history museum. Cut out outlines, as for the invitations, for further decorating. Set up a tent in the backyard to simulate a cave, or have the children make a cave in the bedroom with blankets and sheets. Cut ferns out of green crepe paper.

Favors/Prizes: Small, plastic figures of dinosaurs are available at toy stores to hand out as favors or use as decorations, and larger plastic models can be given as prizes.

Games/Activities: Have a treasure hunt for small, plastic dinosaur figures which you have hidden around the yard.

Play Dinosaur Tag: the one who is "it" is a "dinosaur" and the rest of the children are "cavemen." As the dinosaur tags the other children, they become dinosaurs too, and help chase the remaining cavemen. The last caveman left is the winner.

Show an appropriate movie, such as *One Million Years B.C.*

Food: Serve cold chicken or turkey legs and other food that the children can eat with their hands, with fruit for dessert.

Costumes: Have the children make caveman costumes out of old T-shirts, shorts, and sheets, trimmed with thrift store fur, animal print fabric, or fuzzy throw rugs.

Doll Party

Obviously, this is a party best limited to younger girls. The theme can be presented as the dolls giving a party for the birthday girl, or a birthday party for one of the dolls. If it is done as a party for the dolls, it can be combined with dressing up, so that the children act as adults, giving a party for their "children." In that case, have each guest bring her favorite doll to the party.

Invitations: Buy cute commercial invitations, or make your own, decorating them with pictures of dolls or trimming them with pieces of fabric of the kind used for doll clothes.

Decorations: Decorate one corner of a room as a kind of expanded doll house. Clear out the regular furniture and set it up with any doll furnishing you have or can borrow.

Favors/Prizes: Give each guest a book of paper dolls to cut out and color, and a box of crayons.

Games/Activities: You can keep the girls occupied and amused for some time making their own dolls. These can range from simple puppets to rag dolls. Finger puppets can be made by cutting the fingers out of old gloves (or buy several pair of inexpensive women's gardening gloves). Hand puppets can be made from old socks. In either case, draw faces on the puppets and decorate them with crayons, markers, glue, beads, and scraps of cloth.

For rags dolls, check well ahead of time with your local crafts store or fabric store for patterns and materials. You will probably want to do some of the work, like cutting out the material, ahead of time.

Food: Have a little girl tea party, with child-size versions of fancy sandwiches and cookies, and apple juice in place of tea.

Costumes: If the party is for the dolls, have the girls play dress-up. Otherwise, you may want to have the girls dress up as dolls.

Dress-Up Party

This may be a better theme for little girls than for boys, but properly run, it can be fun for both.

Invitations: These can be handmade, decorating them with pictures cut out of fashion magazines.

Decorations: Don't worry about decorating for this party, except to make the dinner table look very formal and "grown-up" for a tea party or other refreshments.

Favors/Prizes: For a girl's party, get plenty of inexpensive makeup, including a large variety of lipstick and eye shadow. Get enough so that each child has her own.

Games/Activities: Clean out your closets for old clothes, and ask friends and neighbors to help. After the party, the clothes can go to a charity or church organization. The more unusual (for children) the clothes are, the better. Men's hats and suits for boys, and formal dresses for girls, work well to inspire imaginations.

For makeup, buy a lot of inexpensive hypoallergenic makeup products from a discount store, getting a wide range of colors and shades. Get eye shadow, mascara, lipstick, and so on, together with plenty of supplies to put it on and to take it off with (tissues, cotton balls, makeup remover etc.). Provide lots of supervision with makeup, including application lessons. The makeup session can also be done as a Beauty Salon, with the girls making up one another.

The main activity will be the dressing-up itself. You may also want to schedule some "grown-up" games, such as cards, for after the children are all dressed up.

For older children, show a classic movie featuring sophisticated, formal situations, such as *The Philadelphia Story*.

Food: Refreshments can be served as a tea party, with milk in tea cups, and cookies or little cakes on small plates.

Costumes: Half the fun of dressing up is actually putting on the clothes, so either have the children bring the dress-up clothes with them, or provide them yourself. Adult clothes are best, the older, and bigger, the better. For girls, include makeup and hairstyling.

Eskimo Party

This party is best held during the winter. If you live in a warmer climate, you can create a winter scene indoors with white sheets.

Invitations: Cut igloos out of white construction paper and hand letter the invitations on the back.

Decorations: If possible, have the party, or at least part of it, outdoors. If you live in a warm climate or if there is no snow on the ground, you might want to turn one room of your house into a winter land by draping white sheets over chairs and tables, and have the children make igloos under the sheets.

Favors/Prizes: Give small, plastic figures of sled dogs, polar bears, or seals. Try to find inexpensive (or used) books about Eskimos or Arctic explorers.

Games/Activities: Have an Eskimo blanket toss. If you have enough children, divide them into two teams, giving each a blanket and a doll or a stuffed animal. Each team stands around the edges of its blanket and pulls it tight. Place a stuffed animal in the center of each blanket. The children work together to toss the stuffed animal in the air and to catch it again in the blanket. After practicing, see how many times in a row each team can toss the stuffed animal into the air without dropping it. Or have a contest to see how high they can toss the stuffed animal.

Have sled races, with teams running in relays, with the children taking turns pretending to be sled dogs.

If there is snow on the ground, have a snowman-building contest. Or pile the snow into mounds and have the children dig snow caves or "igloos."

Wrap things up with hot chocolate and a movie such as *Call of the Wild,* or a documentary about Eskimos or Arctic exploration.

Food: Real Eskimo food is too hard to get, and too foreign for our tastes. Substitute beef jerky or sausage sticks for whale blubber, and serve snow cones or ice-cream cones for dessert.

Costumes: All bundled up in parkas and snowsuits, the children will look enough like Eskimos.

Farm Party

Invitations: Cut your favorite farm animals out of colored construction paper and hand letter the invitations on the back.

Decorations: Depending on the time of year and the effort involved, you can turn your backyard into a farmyard with a few bales of hay and some corn stalks.

Favors/Prizes: Small, plastic farm animals, toy tractors, or toy pickup trucks all make good favors or treasures to hunt for. The ultimate prizes are the free caps given out by farm equipment manufacturers or herbacide companies.

Games/Activities: "The Farmer in the Dell" is a must. "Hot Potato" is another good game. Play "Johnny-Jump-Up," with the children pretending to be various farm crops. Instructions for all of these games are to be found in the chapter on "Games and Activities" in this book.

Food: Lots of it, including corn on the cob, pitchers of cold milk, and lots of fruit.

Costumes: Old clothes are required, bib overalls being the best thing possible. Otherwise, jeans, a flannel shirt, boots, and a cap, preferably with some kind of emblem or advertising on the front, complete the outfit.

Firehouse Party

Invitations: Type out the invitations on standard 8 ½ x 11″ paper. One at a time, carefully touch a lit match to the corner of the paper and blow it out immediately, so the paper is slightly charred at the edge.

Decorations: Try to find pictures of fire trucks. Hang a map of the city on the wall, and stick multicolored pins in it for "Fire Central."

Favors/Prizes: Get some fire safety brochures from your local fire department and give them out to the children to take home.

Games/Activities: Have an actual firefighter come and talk to the children about fire safety.

Play horseshoes, and have a checker tournament.

Play firefighter's race, a variation on relay races. Divide the children into two or more teams, giving each team a small glass or paper cup to carry water. Start each team with a full glass of water. The first member for each team runs to the other end of the yard and dumps the water into the team's bucket or other container (make sure that all the containers are the same size). They then return to the starting line and hand the glass to the next team member, who fills the glass from a common water source or with a garden hose. The first team to fill its bucket is the winner.

Show an appropriate movie, such as *Backdraft*. (This film might be too intense for younger children.)

Food: Lots of soup or chili, served out of a big pot.

Costumes: Have the children dress up as firefighters with as many items of dark blue clothing as possible.

Fishing Party

If your guest-of-honor loves to fish, this party can be an actual fishing trip for a few friends. Otherwise, turn a home party into a fishing trip.

Invitations: Cut fish outlines from construction paper and write the invitations on them.

Decorations: Cut out additional fish outlines when doing the invitations, and stick them up on the walls. Get travel posters featuring fishing scenes and wildlife posters with pictures of whales or big game fish.

Favors/Prizes: Give out small items of fishing gear (lures, line, etc.) if the children actually fish. Otherwise, get pictures, posters, books, keychains, etc., with a fish theme.

Games/Activities: Play "Bottle Ring" (the directions are in the Games and Activities chapter of this book). Or change "Bottle Ring" to a fishing game by replacing the ring with a hook made of a wire coat hanger. Have the children fish for small packages, each with a loop made of plastic, wire, or pipe cleaners.

Play "Go Fish." The directions are in the "Cards and Dice Games" section of this book.

Wrap things up by showing a movie, such as *Moby Dick* for older children, or a documentary about the sea.

Food: Fish, of course. Have fish sticks or fish sandwiches.

Costumes: If any of the guests or their parents actually fish, the children can dress up as fishermen, complete with rod, reel, and hip waders if desired. Otherwise, get some old clothes from the thrift store and turn them into fishing outfits with a few fishing flies stuck into a vest, or jeans tucked into a pair of high rubber boots.

Giant Party

There are two ways to do this party: either the children are giants, and everything around them is small, or they are in a giant land, with everything outsized. Or combine the two concepts, suggesting that the children are alternately growing and shrinking.

Invitations: Get large sheets of paper (11″ x 17″ or larger) from an office supply store. Hand letter the invitations with a large black marker, making the letters as large as possible.

Decorations: Find very large or very small examples of normal household things at thrift stores and place them around the house. (Small is easier, using doll house furniture, children's play pots and pans, etc.)

Favors/Prizes: Give away the decorations discussed above. For small children, give out copies of fairy tales, or "Jack and the Beanstalk."

Games/Activities: Play "Mother May I," with lots of giant steps or baby steps. Play "Giant Tag," where the child who is "it" is a "giant." As other children are tagged, they become giants too, helping to tag the others, until only one child is left.

Wrap things up with an appropriate movie, such as *Honey, I Shrunk the Kids*.

Food: Serve most anything, in very small or very large portions. Use saucers or serving platters for dinner plates.

Costumes: Have the children wear clothes that are way too big for them, to suggest that they are wearing giant clothes, or way too small, to suggest that they are giants.

Hat Party

Invitations: Draw the outline of a top hat on construction paper, cut it out, and write the invitation on it. Explain the idea in the invitations, and tell the children what to wear.

Decorations: Visit the thrift stores in your area and buy most of the hats you can find, going for variety. Hang the hats around the house and put them on any available surface.

Favors/Prizes: The prizes are hats, of course. Check into having baseball caps or ski hats personalized with the children's names or initials.

Games/Activities: You have to have a Mexican hat dance, of course. You can also come up with several variations on the game of "Hat Toss." These include tossing things (playing cards, for example) into a hat, or tossing a hat over something.

Have a hat contest, with prizes for the largest, smallest, ugliest, and best-decorated hat.

Wind it up with a showing of the movie classic, *Top Hat*.

Food: Bake cookies in the shape of hats, or make hats by placing a cupcake upside down on a large cookie.

Costumes: Hats, yours or theirs.

Haunted House Party

Invitations: Cut out invitations in the form of ghosts, a scary doorway, a cob-webbed window, or other appropriate scene.

Decorations: Get out your Halloween decorations, and look for movie posters for horror films such as the *Halloween* or *Friday the 13th* series. Hang toy spiders from ceiling.

Favors/Prizes: Get lots of inexpensive little magic tricks and gross gag gifts from a toy store.

Games/Activities: Play Gossip in a darkened room. The children sit in a circle, and you start by whispering a sentence, something about ghosts or monsters, in the ear of the first child. That child whispers the same sentence in the ear of the next child, and so on all the way around the circle. The last child says it aloud, and you then read aloud what the original sentence was, which will be quite different.

Wrap things up with a good horror movie.

Food: Serve chicken wings and drumsticks, making up a story about what these are actually pieces of, if that isn't too gross for the younger children.

Costumes: Have the children dress up as ghosts and goblins.

Hawaii Party

Invitations: Get a stack of Hawaii travel brochures from a travel agent or an airline, and paste your invitations inside.

Decorations: Hang leis on the walls, as well as travel posters with beaches and surfing scenes. Decorate with any water sports equipment, such as snorkeling gear.

Favors/Prizes: Get a lot of inexpensive leis, enough for several for each child.

Games/Activities: Find or make some grass skirts and have a hula contest.

Show a Hawaii travel documentary, or Elvis Presley in *Blue Hawaii*.

Food: Be as adventuresome as you want to here, serving anything from pineapple juice to poi.

Costumes: Have the children dress as tourists, including bright print shirts, and cameras hanging from the neck.

Hippie Party

Invitations: Decorate hand-lettered invitations with peace symbols and other designs from the sixties.

Decorations: Decorate the walls with posters and album covers of Sixties rock bands. Keep the lights low, play music from the Sixties, and burn incense.

Favors/Prizes: Pick up a bunch of old record albums from a used record store. The weirder the cover, the better.

Games/Activities: Have the children make their own necklaces or head bands with string, cloth, and lots of beads.

For older children, show an appropriate movie from the period, such as *Woodstock*.

Food: Serve a typical mixed-up menu of beans and rice for dinner and lots of junk food for dessert.

Costumes: Have the children dress as hippies. Tie-dyed shirts are coming back and should be available. Anything old works well as a costume, the older the better, and worn in the layered look. Floor-length skirts are good for the girls, and work shirts or pieces of military uniforms for the boys. Have everyone wear lots of beads and sunglasses.

Hobo party

Invitations: If possible, get a train schedule and write the invitations on photocopies. Otherwise, write the invitation in black marker on old sheets of newspaper.

Decorations: It is best to have the party in the back yard if possible. Build a fire in a barbecue pit or grill. Place a ring of old chairs and lawn furniture in a circle around the fire. If you have firewood, put a few unsplit logs on end to serve as stools.

Favors/Prizes: Give each child a brightly colored bandanna.

Games/Activities: There are a lot of games that can be

played while sitting in a circle. Some of those discussed in the "Games and Activities" chapter of this book include "Gossip," "Ha-Ha-Ha," and "Find the Leader." You can also divide the children into teams and have a scavenger hunt, sending them out to look for empty cans, old newspaper, and so on.

Food: Make stew or chili, and serve it in old, mismatched bowls you picked up at a thrift store. Serve hot chocolate in equally unmatched mugs and coffee cups. Serve the food from a table set up outside your back door, and let the children eat while sitting around the fire in the backyard.

Costumes: Old clothes, the tattier the better.

Jungle Party

Invitations: Trace outlines of jungle animal, such as elephants and giraffes, on construction paper. Cut them out and write your invitations on them.

Decorations: If possible, create a camp in the backyard with several tents. For an indoors party, hang up pictures or posters of jungle animals.

Favors/Prizes: Get a large assortment of small, inexpensive animal figures.

Games/Activities: For a long party, include a trip to the zoo. Have a safari in the back yard or in a local park, including hunting for hidden animal models following treasure maps or clues.

Wrap things up with one of the several dozen *Tarzan* movies (but not the one with Bo Derek).

Food: Have plenty of bananas and more exotic fruit for snacks.

Costumes: The children can dress up as hunters, native guides, or tourists, using old clothes from their parents' closet or from the thrift store.

King's (Queen's) Court Party

Invitations: Cut shields out of colored construction paper. Decorate the front with crayons or markers, and write the invitations on the back.

Decorations: Make bigger shields out of construction paper to hang on the walls. If possible, hang appropriate throw rugs on the walls to simulate tapestries.

Favors/Prizes: Decks of cards carry out the royalty theme. Or have "royal" costume jewelry, such as tiaras and necklaces.

Games/Activities: Have each child make a crown out of construction paper, foil, and sequins.

Divide the children into teams and have a treasure hunt, following hidden clues, for the Holy Grail (a thrift store wine glass or goblet, decorated with beads and sequins).

Wrap up with a rented video such as *Ivanhoe* or *Camelot*.

Food: Serve turkey legs and drinks in large cups or glasses suggestive of goblet.

Costumes: Regal robes can be approximated with full-length bathrobes trimmed with thrift store fur, animal print fabric, or pieces of fuzzy throw rugs.

Library Party

A party with a library theme is a fun way to get kids "hooked on books" at an early age. A visit to the library, especially to the children's section, will give you lots of good ideas for invitations and decorations. If your library regularly has programs for children, the librarian in charge of those will probably have some ideas for library-related activities that children enjoy.

Invitations: Invitations can be made to resemble a library card or overdue notice. A more elaborate invitation could be a small book. You can make a "book" with a construction paper cover and pages stapled in, or you could look for some of the smaller blank books that are now available, and write the invitation in the front of it. Each guest would then have the book as a favor and could use it as an autograph book or diary.

Decorations: Look around your library for ideas. You and your child could reproduce the covers of some favorite books with colored markers on poster board. Put up some appropriate signs such as "QUIET," "BOOK RETURN," "CHECK-OUT," and the like. And, of course, have lots of books and magazines all around.

Favors/Prizes: Of course, natural favors and prizes would be books, bookmarks, or magazines. The bookmarks can be purchased or handmade.

Other fun favors would be inexpensive rubber stamps and ink pads (for older kids only!). These can be the adjustable date stamps, or a variety of others which are available featuring subjects ranging from flowers to animals to cartoon characters.

Games/Activities: Have a book trivia quiz. Find out in advance what popular books most of the children are familiar with, and come up with some easy questions. Play "Overdue Book Return": have a drawing of due-dates, the winner is the one whose book is not overdue. Invite guests to bring along a favorite book to share with others during a story time. (This would be a good wind-down activity at the end of the party.)

A craft activity would be to make a book, or make bookmarks from construction paper or other materials.

Food: Library paste (soft cream cheese) and book worms (candy worms) are fun foods for a library party. A layer cake can be decorated to look like a stack of books, or sheet cake can be decorated to look like a favorite book or magazine cover.

Costumes: A library party might not lend itself to costumes as well as other theme parties. The costumes would either be very subtle or rather complex. So whether to make it a costume party will depend on the age group involved, and how much time you and your guests want to devote to costumes.

On the subtle end is dressing as librarians, which, now that the old-maid librarian stereotype is outdated would mean wearing just about anything.

On the more complex end would be having guests come as their favorite book, or a character out of their favorite book.

Magic Party

Kids love magic, and a magic party is a natural choice if you are going to have a magician entertain. Magic is a popular hobby, so if you ask around you might be able to find a good magician who does magic just for the enjoyment of it, and would be willing to appear for free. Ask around at shops which sell magic supplies for recommendations.

Invitations: Make black top hat-shaped envelopes out of construction paper and cut out white rabbit shapes to write the invitations on. Put the rabbits into the hats, and maybe include a little magic wand (a toy wand, a swizzle stick, or something similar) with instructions for the guests to pull the rabbit out of the hat.

Decorations: Playing cards are easy to draw using black and red markers on poster boards. Aces and low cards such as Twos and Threes are very easy to make. The more ambitious and talented might want to try Kings, Queens, and Jacks. Top hats and rabbits also make good decoration items for a magic theme.

Favors/Prizes: Small, inexpensive magic tricks are available at most hobby shops and craft stores: regular or miniature decks of cards; magic wands; magic scarves.

Games/Activities: If possible, find a magician to perform, or learn a few simple tricks to demonstrate and teach the guests. Give small, inexpensive magic tricks as favors to each guest, and have each perform the trick.

Get a book of card tricks for yourself and learn several easy tricks that you can teach the children. Give each child a deck of cards to keep, and teach them the tricks. For older children, include written instructions on how to do the tricks.

Food: Cut vegetables such as carrots and celery into long "magic wands," and serve with a "secret potion" dip. Party mix, nuts, or candy can be served in magician's hats. Make a cake with cards on top, or in the form of a magician's assistant cut in half.

Costumes: The guests can dress as magicians with a simple paper or cellophane top hat, bow tie, and magic wand.

Mother Goose Party

Very young kids like nursery rhymes, and the nursery rhyme characters can provide a wonderful party theme.

Invitations: Mother Goose invitations can be easily based on any of the characters or stories: shoe-shaped with yarn laces for the Woman Who Lived in the Shoe; spider-shaped for Little Miss Muffet. The choices are many and obvious. Look through your Mother Goose books for plenty of ideas.

Decorations: As with the invitations, decoration ideas are plentiful with a quick look through a Mother Goose book. Hang rubber spiders from the ceiling, á la Miss Muffet.

Favors/Prizes: Mother Goose books or coloring books, and nursery rhyme toy characters.

Games/Activities: Choose some games from Chapter 3 and adapt them to the theme. For example "Simon Says" would become "Mother Goose Says."

Food: How many kids have actually eaten curds and

whey? Why not serve it at your party? Curds can be cottage cheese, perhaps dressed up with some food color or French dressing, and for whey·you can serve milk. The cake can be decorated with one or several Mother Goose characters or themes.

Costumes: Costumes can be of any nursery rhyme character: Simple Simon, Little Miss Muffet, etc. Again, a look through the book will give you plenty of costume and character ideas.

Movie Party

If you have a big screen television, you're in good shape to have a party with a movie theme. But even more fun will be to borrow or rent an actual movie projector and screen to set up a real "theater." See if your library or school lends films and projectors; many libraries have switched to videotapes, but lots of them still have collections of films. If you can't find equipment and films to borrow, look in the Yellow Pages under "Audio-Video Equipment Rental." For younger kids, a feature film will be too long. Rent or borrow some cartoons or short subjects. Have ushers and a concession stand.

Invitations: Movie party invitations can be in the shape of a movie ticket, or made up to look like a movie poster, with the feature "starring" the guest of honor.

Decorations: Decorate with movie posters, rope off some areas, and have an usher admit the guests to the main "theater" where the party will occur. See if there are paper plates and other decorations available for the theme of the latest popular movie in your child's group.

Favors/Prizes: Look for trading cards or small inexpensive merchandise tied in to a movie currently popular with the age group of the guests. It might be a cartoon character, a super hero, a monster, or some other fictional character. Generally, hit movies generate plenty of promotional items, from pencils to T-shirts to drinking glasses.

Games/Activities: Have a movie trivia contest, but be careful to limit the questions to movies appropriate to the age group involved. Have the kids draw movie posters for their favorite films, and give prizes for each.

Food: These days you can get just about any kind of fast food at a movie theater. Set up a "concession stand" and give the guests play money to line up and "buy" their treats. You can have cardboard trays already set up with a hot dog, popcorn, candy, a paper cup of pop, and other snack bar items all ready.

Costumes: Any and all favorite movie characters are fair game for costumes. You can usually find ready-made costumes for characters from movies which are currently hot.

Mystery Party (Detective)

Solving a mystery is always fun and exciting. Have your guests be detectives solving a mystery during the party, such as "The Case of the Missing Birthday Cake."

Invitations: You can make invitations to look like a "Wanted" poster, or make them in the shape of magnifying glass or a Sherlock Holmes style of hat. Invite guests to help solve "The Case of the Missing Birthday Cake," or whatever mystery you invent.

Decorations: Large "Wanted" posters, signs to make the party area look like part of a police station or private detective's office.

Favors/Prizes: Check out a novelty shop or toy store for appropriate equipment: small magnifying glasses, disguises, fingerprinting kits, detective badges, and the like.

Games/Activities: Set up clues and have guests solve

the mystery. Have the guests, or some helpers, play different characters as they act out the mystery and reveal the location of the cake.

If the children are old enough, wrap up the party with a video of a classic "whodunit."

Food: Look for some do-it-yourself fortune cookies, or make your own, and put clues inside. Decorate the cake with appropriate symbols—magnifying glass, badge, fingerprints, and so on.

Costumes: Private eye outfits (hats and trench coats), police uniforms (dark blue shirts and pants), criminal costumes (masks), or prisoner uniforms (striped pants and shirt) can all fit into this theme.

Olympics Party

For an Olympics Party, stress the ceremonial aspects of the event, perhaps with elaborate opening and closing ceremonies, and of course an official Olympic celebration (with cake and goodies). You can specify any type of competition you like, so consider making the "competition" one at which all the guests can be successful. Make a "Party Games Olympics," and select a variety of games in which all guests can score enough points to win a medal.

You can also base your theme on the ancient Olympics, and bring in the Greek gods.

Invitations: The invitation can be an official-looking "Qualifying Certificate" that the guest has been selected to participate in the official ceremonies.

Decorations: Decorate with Olympic torches, laurel wreaths, and Olympic medals.

Favors/Prizes: Olympic "medals" of plastic or candy; fancy personalized scrolls and certificates; prizes related to the various competitions.

Games/Activities: See Chapter 3 for a selection of

games, and choose several to include in your "Party Games Olympics," or adapt several of the games to fit an ancient Olympics theme.

Have a "decathlon," with several contests or races, awarding points for top finishers in each. The one with the most points is the decathlon winner.

Divide the children into teams and run relay races of various kinds.

Food: For an ancient Olympics theme, you could serve "ambrosia," the mythical food of the gods. The ambrosia could be a rich, fragrant punch, a milk shake or blended fruit drink, a pudding, or anything else that suits your imagination. A Mount Olympus cake could have white frosting peaks, or a simple Olympic sheet cake could have Olympic "medals" on top (either candy medalions, decorated cookies, or drawn on with frosting).

Costumes: For a modern Olympics, guests could dress as their favorite Olympic athlete, or just in athletic costumes. For an ancient Olympics, they could dress as ancient Greeks.

Pajama Party

Kids love pajama parties. They get to sleep away from home and stay up late. But they can be a lot of work for parents. Keep the guest list small, limited to very close friends, and all of the same gender.

Invitations: Make the invitation in the shape of a pajama top, glue on a pocket, and slip the invitation into the pocket. Another idea is to make the invitation in the shape of a bed and have the invitation revealed when the sheet is pulled down. Or make the invitation in the shape of an alarm clock.

Decorations: You don't need a lot of decorations, since the main attraction of the party is the sleep-over. Just make the setting festive with some balloons, banners, and crepe paper. Let the guest of honor express some individual personality through the decorations.

Favors/Prizes: Visit the "travel size" section of a large drug store or discount store and assemble little overnight kits for the guests. Items might include a travel toothbrush, comb, and travel sizes of soaps and other toiletries as appropriate for boys or girls. For larger prizes, maybe an inexpensive alarm clock (an old-fashioned, wind-up style is fun).

Games/Activities: Such a small group will be able to provide its own entertainment to a great extent. Let the birthday child set the direction—maybe renting some favorite videos, or video games. Discuss what the group will do for the evening, and provide any resources needed. Have some back-up ideas, such as some games from Chapter 3 ready, in case the group gets bored.

Food: Serve snacks and birthday cake at night, and a fun breakfast in the morning. See Chapter 8 for some breakfast items including coffee cakes, pancakes, and blended juice drinks.

Costumes: Wear anything, then change into pajamas, naturally.

Parade Party

A parade party can be fun for younger children. Have the guests decorate their bikes or wagons, or build floats or form a "marching band" to have a parade in the neighborhood in honor of the birthday. The birthday child can be the "grand marshall" or lead the parade. Have a reviewing stand with judges to give awards for the best entry in certain categories. Have enough categories so each guest wins a prize.

Get a tape of marching band music to play on a portable stereo during the parade, and during the party. Check with your public library music collection.

Invitations: Make the invitation look like a handbill announcing the big parade coming to town.

Decorations: Have plenty of materials available—balloons, crepe paper, pinwheels, paper flowers, and more—for the guests to decorate their bikes or themselves for the parade. The same materials can be used to decorate the house.

Favors/Prizes: You might look for inexpensive toy band instruments, or even kazoos. Toy twirling batons or drum major staffs would be fun prizes.

Games/Activities: The major activity will be the parade itself. Follow the parade with the awarding of prizes, then the food and the rest of the party. Have some general games and activities ready to keep everyone entertained if the other activities don't fill the allotted party time.

Food: Set up a concession stand or food wagon at the "parade grounds" and serve hot dogs, pop, popcorn, and similar treats. The birthday cake can be decorated as a parade float.

Costumes: The guests pretty much decorate themselves as part of their floats, or they can dress as band members, honor guard members, or drill team members.

Pet Party

At a pet party, guests can pretend they are a cat or dog.

Invitations: Cut out the invitations in the shape of a dog or cat, a dog biscuit, or a dog house. Draw in the appropriate details, and leave space for the invitation information.

Decorations: Make a dog house out of an appliance box, and have the guests crawl in to find treats. Have plenty of stuffed dogs and cats around, or posters of dogs and cats.

Favors/Prizes: Small stuffed animals, small plastic dogs and cats.

Games/Activities: Many standard games can be adapted to a pet party; browse through Chapter 3 for ideas. As an example, "Simon Says" can become "Rover Says." The game of "Hide and Seek" can be "Lost Puppies" or "Lost Kittens." Instead of "Tag" the game would become "Dog Catcher," and so on. For a quieter wind-down activity, each guest can tell what kind of dog or cat they would like to be, and why, or tell a story about their own dog or cat if they have one.

Food: Cookies or biscuits can be made in bone shapes; granola or party mix can be served from "pet food" containers and eaten from "dog dishes"; for a main course, hot dogs for dogs, tuna fish for cats.

Costumes: Have some face paint for guests to paint on whiskers as appropriate, or look for inexpensive animal masks or noses. Dog and cat masks are simple to make out of construction paper, and dog or cat ears are simple to make out of furry scraps of material attached to an elastic band.

Photo Party

It's fun to take pictures, and to play professional photographer. At a photo party kids get to do that, and have some pictures of their own to take home at the end of the day.

Invitations: Get some inexpensive plastic picture frames, and put the invitations in the frame. Include an actual snapshot pasted onto the invitation, or a picture cut out of a magazine.

If you can't find inexpensive plastic frames, make your own photo mats from poster board. Cut a piece of white board for the bottom to write the invitation on, and put another piece of colored board on top with a cutout to frame the invitation. Here again, you can paste an actual snapshot onto the invitation—a nice picture taken by the birthday child, or a picture of last year's party, or whatever.

Decorations: Paint some large cartons to look like "box cameras." Put up lots of posters, or poster boards covered with snapshots.

Favors/Prizes: Small photo albums or frames. Toy cameras. "Gadget bags" filled with candy or small toy items.

Games/Activities: Have some instant cameras and film, and set up a photo studio where guests can take turns being model and photographer. If you give photo albums as favors, guests can make their own photo album during the party. If you don't have and can't borrow an instant camera, check with a one-hour photo lab about inexpensive, instant processing during the party. A helper can run the film to be developed while the guests eat or do another activity.

Have the guests pose for a group picture, and send a copy to each guest after the party to put in their album.

If you don't have a camcorder, rent one for the occasion. Have the children tape each other, possibly even making up and filming a movie. Play back the videos near the end of the party.

Have the guests pose for a group picture, and send a copy to each guest after the party to put in their album.

Food: Sheet cakes easily lend themselves to decoration as a photo, frame, or piece of film.

Costumes: Have a variety of informal costume items and props available for guests to wear as they model for pictures. Or use a large piece of plywood or cardboard for models to stand behind with a cutout for their faces. Have the guests paint characters or scenes to incorporate the faces, and make photos of each guest.

Pig Party

The pig party is an official okay for kids to be as messy as they want. As such, it is best to hold outdoors, and guests' parents should be warned in advance so that the guests will wear clothes that won't be ruined by stains.

Invitations: Cut out construction paper in the form of a pig, or draw a pig sty. Write the information on the pig, or in the sty. To be more elaborate, put the pig in a cut-out sty.

Decorations: Set up a "pig sty" in the yard with some temporary fencing, or some bales of hay. Have pictures of pigs and other farm animals around.

Favors/Prizes: Toy pigs.

Games/Activities: Have a "Pig Out" contest. Make some soft food (jello is good) and see which pig can finish it first—no hands allowed!

Have a pig relay race. Divide the children into teams. At the signal, the first member of each team runs on all fours to a spot, picks up a small apple in his or her mouth, and, holding the apple in the teeth, runs back on all fours to the starting line. The other team members follow in turn, and the first team through is the winner.

Food: Have plenty of foods which can be eaten with fingers. No spoons or forks for pigs! If you serve a meal, concoct some "pig slop" the pigs can eat directly from the bowls. The sloppier the better! Maybe something like macaroni and cheese or beans and franks (cut up into bite-sized pieces).

Costumes: Make pig snouts and ears from pink construction paper or fabric. Attach them with pieces of elastic.

Pilgrim Party

The early settlers are often associated with Thanksgiving, but they can be called into duty for a party any time of year, especially in the fall.

Invitations: Make the invitations in the shape of a pilgrim hat or bonnet.

Decorations: Old maps of the new world (copy from books or draw on poster boards); dried corn, pumpkins, gourds.

Favors/Prizes: Toy turkeys, toy sailing ships.

Games/Activities: Use one of the old maps to "Pin the Pilgrim on the New World." A version of a treasure hunt could be to find the "new world," a hidden map or globe.

Food: Turkey sandwiches, corn on the cob, candy corn, and pumpkins. Decorate the birthday cake with pilgrim hats, pumpkins, and candy corn.

Costumes: Pilgrim hats and bonnets are easily made from construction paper. Some of the guests may want to be costumed as Native Americans.

Pirate Party

The romance of sailing the high seas can easily be translated into a fun party for kids. Turn your party room into the main deck, and your kitchen into a galley, and set sail!

Invitations: Make invitations in the shape of a ship, a cannon, or a pirate's sword. To be more elaborate, draw a rolling sea on one sheet of paper, and cut a slit along one of the waves to insert the ship with the invitation written on it.

Decorations: Rope, netting, nautical items, a treasure chest, swords, and other pirate items.

Favors/Prizes: Have little treasure chests full of treats, eye patches, bandannas, and toy swords.

Games/Activities: A treasure hunt: make a personalized treasure map and hide a little treasure chest for each guest.

Wrap things up with a classic pirate movie, maybe one with Errol Flynn.

Food: Skewered hot dogs or meatballs. Treasure chests full of snacks. Tankards of Pirate's Punch.

Costumes: An eye patch and a colorful bandanna wrapped

around the head makes an instant pirate out of even the most land-locked child. Eye patches can be easily made from construction paper or black fabric and a piece of elastic or yarn. Buy inexpensive bandannas, or just cut squares of appropriately colorful fabric remnants. Tattered jeans and a rugby shirt complete the costume.

Political Party

A colorful political convention can be fun any time of year, but is most appropriate around election times.

Invitations: Make the invitations look like a political brochure or campaign poster with the guest of honor running for mayor, congress, senate, president, or any other office of choice. Another possibility is an election notice and sample ballot, with the guests listed as candidates for various offices.

Decorations: Plenty of red, white, and blue streamers, bunting, and balloons. Flags. Make big campaign posters and signs. Maybe some delegation signs for a number of states (find out what states your guests were born in, and make signs for those states).

Favors/Prizes: Flags and buttons. Toy elephants and donkeys.

Games/Activities: Have a number of "elections" where guests nominate and vote for favorite things in a number of categories: TV show, singer, movie, food. They can also nominate and vote on least favorite things: class at school, food, chore around the house.

You can make up some ballots in advance for votes on some of the categories, and have the guests at the "convention" nominate in other categories.

Food: Red, white, and blue cake. "Elephant Feed" (trail mix or granola) and "Donkey Drink" (any kind of punch).

Costumes: Funny hats, vests, sashes, political buttons, delegate "credentials" to hang around the neck.

Railroad Party

Many kids today have never been on a passenger train, but are still fascinated by the size and noise of trains. A railroad party gives everyone a chance to be a railroad engineer and enjoy the romance of the rails.

Invitations: The invitation can be a railroad ticket or timetable, or in the shape of a train engine, car, or caboose.

Decorations: Railroad tickets, bells, whistles, signs for the station and the tracks.

Favors/Prizes: Toy or inexpensive pocket watches. Bandanas. Toy train items. Paper punches (ticket punches).

Games/Activities: Make up a "Conductor" quiz game on various train destinations. Make each guest a ticket with several well-known destinations, such as the Grand Canyon or Yellowstone Park. Then the "Conductor" looks at the ticket and asks, "You're going to the Grand Canyon. Do you know what state that's in?" A right answer gets the ticket punched, and guests see who can get the most punches.

Food: Just about any kind of food can be served, but serve it either in the "dining car" or out of "lunch buckets." Decorate the cake with a railroad theme. A layer cake can have toy trains on top, a sheet cake can be decorated as a railroad ticket or other related theme.

Costumes: Engineer caps, red bandannas to wear around the neck, toy pocket watches. Conductor caps and ticket punches.

Rainbow Party

The object of a rainbow party is to celebrate colors. Invite guest to dress in as many different colors as they can.

Invitations: Obviously, the invitations should include a rainbow, along with instructions to wear a lot of colorful clothes.

Decorations: Get as many different colors of party streamers and balloons as you can find. Use crepe paper or other materials to construct a big rainbow.

Favors/Prizes: Rainbow pins and other items. A selection of colorful treats in a colorful bag or other container. A variety of crayons or colored markers. Coloring books.

Games/Activities: Deputize the guests as "Color Police" and give them colorful badges. Give them a list of black and white items that are guilty of not being colorful enough, and have them hunted down. If you use all white items, they can then be colored. Some items you might hide to be colored are plaster figures, plain white T-shirts, or painters caps to be decorated.

Food: Anything colorful! Make a party mix with as many different colored candies as you can find. Various colors of jelly beans. Cubes of different colors of jello mixed together. Make marble cake: Using a white cake batter, divide it in several parts; color each part with different food colorings, then swirl them together before baking.

Costumes: Have each guest wear as many different colors as possible. Give prizes for the most colors, most clashing, most harmonious, and others, so each guest gets a prize.

Restaurant Party

A restaurant party gives guests an opportunity to play chef. It can be more work to let the kids help make the food than if you do it yourself, but it is a rare opportunity for them to get involved in the kitchen.

Invitations: A fancy menu: Fold construction paper in half, put some gold or silver string in the fold, write a fancy name on the front, and list the information inside.

Decorations: Make the party table look like a fancy restaurant with a white tablecloth (paper or plastic!) and fancy-looking (paper or plastic!) place settings and napkins. Have fancy-looking candles and flowers on the table, and menus. You, or a helper, can be a comical, snooty maitre d', or head chef.

Favors/Prizes: Gift certificates for a fast-food restaurant, toy food, and cookware.

Games/Activities: A major activity will be helping to make the food.

Food: Guests help prepare the food. A good choice for this is pizza. Guests might also help decorate the cake.

Costumes: Chef hats, white outfits, white bandannas.

Roots Party

Invite each guest to somehow feature his or her ethnic heritage by wearing a costume or bringing something to show and tell about.

Invitations: The invitation can be based on a map of the world, with the birthday child's roots highlighted.

Decorations: World maps, globes, items representing various cultures.

Favors/Prizes: Maps, toy globes, small ethnic craft items.

Games/Activities: Trace each guest's roots on a map. Have a geography quiz.

Food: Samples of various ethnic foods. Pizza, tacos, fortune cookies, French bread, Scottish shortbread, and others.

Costumes: Put together a costume chest of items representing various cultures (beret, sombrero, kilt) for kids to try on. Have each guest wear something or bring something.

Safari Party

A safari party is a good opportunity for younger kids to show off their entire collections of "wild" stuffed animals.

Older kids can just enjoy the jungle theme.

Invitations: Wild animal themes, jungles, grass huts.

Decorations: Plenty of "wild" stuffed animals, vines hanging from the doorways, posters of wild animals and jungle scenes.

Favors/Prizes: Toy animals, artifacts from Africa.

Games/Activities: Games to identify various jungle animals, a "safari" treasure hunt.

Wrap things up with a jungle movie, possibly one of the old *Tarzan* movies.

Food: Decorate the cake with plastic animals, or with a jungle theme. Construct "grass huts" on the cake with colored coconut shreds.

Costumes: Jungle explorers, big-game hunters, African tribal costumes.

Science Fiction Party

Science fiction seems to keep its popularity year after year; if it's not the crew of a spaceship that kids are crazy about, it's a cuddly extraterrestrial creature. If there's a current science fiction craze, that makes an ideal party theme. If not, there are the classics of space voyages or the "Monster Who Ate Your City."

Invitations: As appropriate, the invitation can be a spaceship, a monster, a map of the universe, or a particular character from a popular science fiction story.

Decorations: Posters of spaceships or characters. Create an imaginary environment to fit the story—a spaceship bridge, alien world, or whatever.

Favors/Prizes: Toy characters, ray guns, model spaceships.

Games/Activities: If the theme revolves around a currently or recently popular film or television show, a trivia game is a good activity. There are often trivia books and games marketed for popular films and shows.

Food: Trail mix or granola can be "Monster Mix." For a space theme, drinks can be served from squeeze bottles and foods such as peanut butter, jelly, and soft cheese spreads can be squeezed from tubes onto bread or crackers. Easy to fill, reusable tubes are used to carry these kinds of foods for camping, and are available from major sporting goods stores.

The cake can be decorated with small, plastic figures, made in the shapes of monsters, or decorated to reflect specific characters.

Costumes: Costumes can be made to match a particular story, or can be based on generic science fiction characters such as robots, spaceship crew members, aliens, monsters, etc.

Science Party

For a group of kids interested in science, this party is a natural; but all kids can be hooked into the fun of being a "mad scientist."

Invitations: Make the invitation in the form of a test tube, microscope, or other scientific item.

Decorations: Decorate with plenty of strange-looking equipment. Build the equipment from old appliances, electronic parts, garden hose—anything that can look strangely scientific.

Favors/Prizes: Small science experiments, books.

Games/Activities: There are plenty of entertaining do-it-yourself science projects and demonstrations which are safe and easy for kids of all ages to participate in. The local library should have plenty of books on the subject.

Food: Serve food "experiments," such as green macaroni and cheese, "mutant hot dogs" (thick slices of bologna grilled, and served like hamburgers, and "Mad Scientist

Punch" (any punch, made a strange color with food coloring, and served from an unusual beaker).

Costumes: Mad scientist costumes: lab coats (old white shirts), glasses, fright wigs.

Sherwood Forest Party

Robin Hood, Maid Marian, and the gang are always favorites with kids, particularly following the latest *Robin Hood* movie.

Invitations: A green archer's hat with feather, a large arrow, a sword, or a castle turret makes a fun Sherwood Forest invitation.

Decorations: Plenty of cardboard for trunks, and green crepe paper for leaves, to make a thick forest; bows and arrows.

Favors/Prizes: Bows and arrows, plastic figurines, feathered caps.

Games/Activities: Have an archery contest, using toy bows and suction-cup arrows.

Have a treasure hunt through "Sherwood Forest."

Play "Cops and Robbers" (see chapter 3), changing the teams to the sheriff's men and the merry men.

Wind down the party with a showing of a Robin Hood video, either the new Kevin Costner version or one of the classics.

Food: Friar Tuck Cider (apple cider), Forest Franks (hot dogs), and a cake decorated with green frosting, trees, or bows and arrows. For a banquet atmosphere, serve fried chicken or turkey legs (no silverware, of course) and tankards of ale (root beer).

Costumes: Green archer costumes, Friar Tuck robes, Maid Marian outfits.

Shipwreck Party

Pirates are always a favorite with kids because of their colorful costumes and even more colorful ways.

Invitations: Your invitations can be in the shape of ships (ship-shape!), a treasure chest, cannon, sword, parrot, keg of rum, or any other nautical theme.

Decorations: Nautical items such as ropes, nets, telescopes, swords.

Favors/Prizes: Toy swords, telescopes, or small treasure chests full of treats.

Games/Activities: A treasure hunt is a natural; make a treasure map for each guest leading to his or her personal treasure chest.

Food: Pirate Punch (any punch), parrot (chicken), dubloons (candy coins, or cookies stamped with a butter or shortbread press), and of course a cake decorated to match the theme.

Costumes: Pirates! Easy to do with some old, ripped shirts, bandannas for the head, and eye patches. Add swords and telescopes, and the kids are ready to sail. Or use tattered shirts and shorts, to simulate shipwreck attire.

Space Party

The adventure of space travel—either the reality of astronauts or the fantasy of science fiction—has an excitement and appeal to it, which makes it an excellent party theme.

Invitations: Make invitations in the shape of a rocket, space capsule, the moon, or planets; include a map of the universe.

Decorations: Maps of the universe, posters, model spaceships.

Favors/Prizes: Maps of the universe, posters of the moon or planets, toy spaceships or astronauts.

Games/Activities: Get a map of the constellations and have kids try to find several of them.

Wind things up with a space movie (one of the *Star Wars* epics, for example) or, for older children, a Carl Sagan documentary.

Food: Drinks can be served from squeeze bottles; foods such as peanut butter, jelly, and soft cheese spreads can be squeezed from tubes onto bread or crackers. Easy to fill, reusable tubes are used to carry these kinds of foods for camping, and are available from many sporting goods stores.

Costumes: Astronaut space suits, space aliens, rocket ships, planets.

Sports Party

Most kids have a sport they are interested in, even if they don't participate. Some popular ones are baseball, football, soccer, gymnastics, skating, basketball, lacrosse, and others. It's easy to build a party around a sports theme, and, for older kids, the party could include an outing to a game. You can plan the party theme around a specific sport, or include all sports so each guest can promote his or her favorite.

Invitations: Sports party invitations can be made to look like a ticket, a program, a scorecard, or made in the shape of an item of equipment: a ball, helmet, bat, or whatever.

Decorations: Posters, equipment, and other items appropriate for the sport or sports being featured. Adult helpers can dress as referees or umpires.

Favors/Prizes: Balls and other sporting equipment. Water bottles, whistles, collector cards and albums, books, videos.

Games/Activities: Board or video versions of the sport being featured. Have an outing to see a real game. Show a "bloopers" or highlights tape for older kids. For younger kids, a toss-the-football or -baseball game.

Food: A home-style meal can be served at the "training table" for a football party. Guests can serve themselves from a large cooler of "sports drink." Snacks can be "hawked" to the crowd, or served from a consession stand—peanuts, popcorn and other ballpark favorites.

Costumes: Appropriate uniforms, whether the party centers on one sport or each guest comes as a favorite sports figure. Related costumes could include drum majors, cheerleaders, coaches, referees, and umpires.

Travel Party

The magic of travel to new, mysterious, and romantic places appeals to young and old, and an imaginary trip is so much easier on everyone.

Invitations: Invitations can resemble an airline or cruise ship ticket, or a passport. If you can get a snapshot of each guest, you can make an individualized passport for each.

Decorations: Travel posters, model planes or ships, maps.

Favors/Prizes: Little travel kits with travel-size items. Books, maps.

Games/Activities: Have a geography contest, with the children answering questions (appropriate to their age), or finding cities or countries on a map or globe.

If you have a computer available (or even better, two computers), buy a copy of one of the "Carmen Sandiego" computer games (such as "Where in the World is Carmen Sandiego?"). Divide the children into teams and see who does best in solving the game.

Food: Have samples of various ethnic cuisines: French,

Italian, Mexican, Greek, and others. Plenty of ethnic cookbooks are available from the library.

Costumes: Costumes might include airline pilots, tour guides, or costumes to represent various exotic destinations.

Western Theme

The wild west still appeals to the imagination, and kids love to put on a western hat, saddle up, and mosey over to the camp fire.

Invitations: Make invitations in the shape of a western hat, a boot, a horse, a covered wagon, a coil of rope, or a cactus.

Decorations: Ropes, bales of hay, a chuck wagon, a campfire.

Favors/Prizes: Lassos, sheriff badges, toy character figures, or horses.

Games/Activities: Roping contest, campfire songs.

Food: Cook over a campfire if possible, or set up a "chuck wagon." Serve food from tin plates and cups.

Costumes: Western hats, bandannas, badges, lassos.

When-I-Grow-Up Party

Kids love to play grown-up, and here's a chance to share the game with their friends and make a party of it. Give kids a chance to think about what they (and the world) will be like in twenty years.

Invitations: Make the invitation look like the calendar for the birthday month in twenty years and circle and mark the birthday: "Lisa's 24th" (or 25th, or 26th, or whatever). You can find a perpetual calendar in many almanacs.

Decorations: Calendars, posters of various professions. Futuristic items.

Favors/Prizes: Calendars, books.

Games/Activities: Make a list of things that weren't invented twenty years ago (videotapes, video games, bank cash machines, CD players, telephone answering machines, personal computers) and list the ones you could give up easily. Predict what things will be invented in the next twenty years.

Food: Make the cake with twenty additional candles, and decorate it for the current age plus twenty years.

Costumes: Costumes should relate to what they want to be when they grow up.

Wizard of Oz Party

Going off to see the Wizard is a great excuse for a party, and the story has some favorite colorful characters to inspire fun costumes and games.

Invitations: Cut ruby slippers from red construction paper, and glue on red glitter; or do an invitation with a "yellow brick road" on it.

Decorations: Set up a yellow brick road from the front door to the party area. Make a sign welcoming visitors to Oz. Make a crepe paper tornado near the front door, with a hidden fan—to "blow" the guests into Oz. Design a crepe paper rainbow.

Favors/Prizes: Rainbow pins, stickers. Colored markers, coloring books.

Games/Activities: Play "Follow the Leader" as "Follow the Yellow Brick Road." "Pin the Hat" (or Broom) on the witch. Other games from Chapter 3, using characters and themes from Oz.

End the party with a showing of the movie.

Food: Rainbow sherbet, any other foods which can be colored in rainbow hues. Decorate the cake with a rainbow or a yellow brick road.

Costumes: Dorothy, witches, Tin Man, Scarecrow, Lion.

Wrong Season Party

Kids like to be absurd sometimes, and a Wrong Season party lets them indulge that inclination. Besides, a Wrong Season party is fun for adults too. Some ideas for Wrong Season parties are to have Christmas or Halloween in the summer, or a beach party in winter.

Invitations: Make the invitation match the Wrong Season theme you have chosen: a Christmas card for your party in July, for example.

Decorations: Decorate to match the theme: Christmas decorations, or beach chairs and umbrellas.

Favors/Prizes: Christmas trinkets, beach toys, whatever is appropriate (or inappropriate, actually!).

Games/Activities: Choose activities to fit the wrong season, such as Christmas carols in summer or beach volleyball in winter.

Food: Christmas cookies and candies, candy canes, hot chocolate; or hot dogs and lemonade. Whatever is wrong for the season. Decorate the cake appropriately.

Costumes: Out of season clothes, or appropriate costumes if you do something like Halloween in the spring or summer.

Zoo Party

A zoo party can include an actual trip to the zoo, if you have one nearby. Otherwise, it is fun for kids to pretend to be a favorite wild animal.

Invitations: Make the invitation in the shape of a favorite zoo resident, or use some postcards from the zoo. Another choice would be to get a lot of animal stickers and create a small zoo on each invitation.

Decorations: Plenty of posters of zoo animals, plenty of stuffed animals.

Favors/Prizes: Plastic animals, zoology books, coloring books.

Games/Activities: Have children identify various zoo animals. Play "Animal Trainer" (see the chapter on Games and Activities).

Wrap things up with a wildlife documentary.

Food: Feature zoo food: set up a concession stand for hot dogs, peanuts, popcorn, and other zoo favorites. Or make "Monkey Milkshakes" (banana shake), "Zoo Milk" (see recipes, Chapter 8), and other foods given exotic, zoo-related names.

Costumes: Guests can come as, or make simple costumes to be their favorite zoo animal.

Holiday
and Other Themes

If your child's birthday falls near a holiday, you might want to have a party using that theme.

Or, you might just want an excuse to throw a party as a reward for some special accomplishment. Here are some general party "excuses." More detailed holiday party plans are on the following pages.

Monthly Theme Ideas

Here are some usual and less usual days to consider for a party theme throughout the year.

January
   1   New Year's Day
   6   12th Day of Christmas (Three Kings Day)
   9   Sherlock Holmes' Birthday
   15   Martin Luther King Day
   19   Edgar Allan Poe's Birthday
       Super Bowl Sunday

February

2   Groundhog Day
14   Valentine's Day
President's Day, 3rd Monday

March

2   Dr. Seuss' Birthday, 1904
6   Michelangelo's Birthday, 1475
16   First rocket launched, 1926
17   St. Patrick's Day
21   Vernal Equinox (First Day of Spring)
Easter
Purim

April

1   April Fools' Day
23   Shakespeare's Birthday
Arbor Day, last Friday

May

1   May Day
Kentucky Derby
Memorial Day, last Monday
Mother's Day, second Sunday

June

14   Flag Day
21   Summer Solstice (First Day of Summer)
Father's Day, third Sunday

July

1   Dominion Day in Canada
4   Independence Day in United States
14   Bastille Day in France
21   Neil Armstrong is first man on the moon, 1969

August

13   Alfred Hitchcock's Birthday, 1899

September

8   First *Star Trek* episode aired, 1966
16   Independence Day in Mexico

22 Autumn Equinox (First Day of Autumn)
  Labor Day, first Monday
  Rosh Hashanah

October
31 Halloween
  Columbus Day, second Monday
  Canadian Thanksgiving, second Monday

November
11 Veterans Day
  Thanksgiving, fourth Thursday

December
 5 Walt Disney's Birthday, 1901
17 Wright Brothers Day (first flight, 1903)
21 Winter Solstice (First Day of Winter)
24 Christmas Eve
25 Christmas
  Hanukkah

April Fools' Day

This is a good excuse to just have fun. An April Fools' Party can also be a theme party, such as a Backward Party or a Wrong Season Party, which are described in the "Theme and Holiday Parties" chapter of the book.

Invitations: Just about anything goes here. Use old birthday or Christmas cards, baby shower invitations, or anything else you have around or can buy cheap.

Decorations: Clean out the attic or basement, and decorate the house with all those things that you have gotten for gifts over the years and never displayed in public. The worse it looks the better.

Favors/Prizes: Give away the decorations, so you don't have to put them back in the attic.

Games/Activities: Play standard games that everyone knows, such as "Hide-and-Seek," but change the rules, with or without telling the children ahead of time. Or change the rules in the middle of the game. Have a relay race, with the prize going to the slowest team. (This race should be run over a very short distance, and no fair stopping.) Have a treasure hunt with some terrible prizes. Whoever finds a prize gets to make someone else take it.

Food: Arrange ahead of time for pizza to be delivered, and for the pizzeria to send along an extra empty box or two. With the children seated at the table, open the pizza box in which there is moldy bread or one slice of pizza or nothing.

Costumes: Have a contest for the ugliest shirt, the worst-fitting outfit, or the most mismatched ensemble.

Back to School

One approach is to have a party commemorating the death of summer. This is more appropriate for older children who will appreciate the humor and irony of the concept and the gags throughout the party. For younger children, make it more positive, helping them look forward to what the school year will bring.

Invitations: If possible, have very somber invitations done on a computer and laser printer, using large black type and heavy black borders.

Decorations: Drape the house with a lot of black crepe paper. Put vases of dead, dried flowers around. Hang posters of beach scenes or summer activities and drape them with black streamers.

Favors/Prizes: School supplies, such as pens, pencils, or rulers, can be wrapped in black paper and tied with black ribbon.

Games/Activities: Have words games, spelling bees, math contests, and other activities with ties to schooling.

Food: Serve cafeteria-style food, preferably on trays, or at least on paper plates with individual compartments.

Costumes: Children can dress either in something very obvious as a back to school outfit, or in mourning.

Christmas

A Christmas Party is expected to follow certain guidelines, but there is room for some creativity within the traditional bounds.

Invitations: The party invitations should be traditional, either purchased or handmade. Make your own invitations by decorating a sheet of colored paper with cut-out snow flakes. Or use cookie cutters to draw outlines of stars, Christmas trees, or Santas on heavy colored paper, cut them out, and paste them on heavy white paper for invitations.

Decorations: Deck the house with traditional Christmas decorations, or have the children make the decorations as part of the party.

Favors/Prizes: Candy canes and Christmas cookies are old-hat, but expected. Any small toys of the "stocking stuffer" variety are appreciated, particularly if nicely wrapped.

Games/Activities: Have the children put together decorations for the party or to take home. Pop up a big batch of popcorn and have the children make long strings of popcorn with a needle and thread. Cut out strips of colored paper, ½" to 1" wide and 8" to 10" long. Put a dab of glue on one end of a strip and form a ring. Repeat with another color, passing it through the first ring before gluing it. Add more and more links to form a chain that can be draped on the tree or over a doorway.

An alternative to the constant food and gifts of the season is to have each child bring an old toy no longer played with. The toys can be wrapped and given to one of the many toy drives for underprivileged children going on at Christmas time.

For a pre-Christmas party, have plenty of colored paper, particularly red and green, and other craft materials on hand. Let the children make Christmas cards for family and friends.

Wrap up with an appropriate video, such as *A Christmas Carol*.

Food: Here again, it is hard to buck, or to beat, tradition. Milk and Christmas cookies are an eagerly anticipated snack, as are holiday candies.

Costumes: Costumes can be an unwanted extra burden or expense for parents at Christmas, so try to keep it simple if you feel the need for costumes. Options include dressing as Santa's elves, characters from the Dickens era, or present-day carolers.

Cinco de Mayo

Cinco de Mayo is Spanish for "Fifth of May," a Mexican holiday commemorating the defeat of Napolean's invading army.

Invitations: Decorate invitations with the Mexican flag, or deliver a bag or basket of tortilla chips with the invitation written on the bag.

Decorations: Travel posters of Mexico, plenty of colorful crepe paper, and, if you can find or make one, a piñata. Make a piñata with papier-mâché and fill it with candy and other small treats.

Favors/Prizes: Posters, books, sombreros, small jars of salsa and small bags of tortilla chips, Mexican candy (see if your community has a Mexican grocery).

Games/Activities: Break the piñata. Have a Mexican geography quiz.

Food: Mexican food, of course! Kids love tacos, burritos, chips, and salsa.

Costumes: Traditional Mexican costume—hats, serapes.

Columbus Day

Columbus Day is a holiday that is celebrated less and less every year, but it is a good opportunity to combine some fun and some history. You might want to use this occasion to put the Columbus legend into perspective, and to provide younger children with a more accurate picture of the European settlement of America.

Invitations: Photocopy an early map of the New World from a historic atlas. Write the invitations on the copies with colored markers, drawing a large "X" at your approximate location on the map.

Decorations: Decorate with pictures of old sailing ships, early maps of the New World, and any items or pictures suggesting the early European explorations of America.

Favors/Prizes: Give out copies of old maps of the New World, books about Columbus, or books about Native Americans and early European and Scandinavian voyages to America.

Games/Activities: Divide the children into teams and have each team follow a series of hidden clues in search of a passage to India (the front door, leading to refreshments).

Food: Serve "grog" (fruit punch) and beef jerky to represent the days of hardship at sea on the old ships. Follow with a cake decorated with little plastic sailing ships on an endless sea.

Costumes: Have the children dress up as sailors or as Native Americans.

Earth Day

Earth Day is a good opportunity to combine fun with lessons about the environment, and to teach children the need for concern about the earth. One approach is to treat it as a birthday party for Mother Earth.

Invitations: Write the invitations on recycled paper, such as the back of computer printouts or cut-up brown paper grocery bags.

Decorations: Hang posters with pictures of the earth taken from space or pictures of natural beauty, such as forests or rivers. You can contrast these with pictures of clear-cut forest land or polluted air, if you can find them.

Favors/Prizes: As much as possible, everything at the party should be recycled. Give books or toys which other children no longer use, stressing the good to be derived by reusing them rather than throwing them away.

Games/Activities: Have a nature scavenger hunt to make the children more aware of the world around them. If possible, have the activities outdoors, in as natural an environment as possible. (Keep in mind the need for close supervision as the environment gets less and less familiar to the children.) Divide the children into teams and have them plant several trees in your back yard or in a local park.

Food: Serve healthy foods and snacks, avoiding meat if possible and substituting fruit for cake or candy.

Costumes: Have the children dress for the outdoors. With jeans and workshirts and boots or old shoes, they can pretend to be forest rangers while they play in the woods or plant trees.

Easter

Invitations: Use commercial invitations, or make your own using cut-out pictures of little bunnies and chicks.

Decorations: Young children still respond to the traditional Easter bunnies and chicks. Decorate with large pictures or posters of these animals. Hang streamers of bright spring-colored paper around the house.

Favors/Prizes: A small basket with some jelly beans and a chocolate rabbit for each child is plenty.

Games/Activities: An Easter-egg hunt is a must. If possible, start out the party with the children dyeing Easter eggs. Let the eggs dry and have an accomplice hide them while you are directing other activities. Make sure that there are enough eggs to go around, and hold a few back for those who don't find any. Follow this up by having an egg-roll race, with each child pushing an egg across the floor by hand, with a spoon, or with his or her nose. This race can be on an individual basis, or with the children divided into two or more teams.

Food: This is traditionally a high-calorie day. Counter the trend by serving some light snacks, such as fruit, although a few jelly beans or small chocolate rabbits are obligatory.

Costumes: Dress-up clothes à la *Easter Parade* are too easily dirtied or damaged, particularly in an egg hunt. Casual clothes are best for this one.

Flag Day

Flag Day is not a major holiday, and many children will not recognize it as such. It is a good chance to have fun, to teach some history, and to break up the summer.

Invitations: Make your own invitations, decorating them with small flag stickers or with various combinations of red, white, and blue colors.

Decorations: Flags, of course. Lots of flags, including as many previous versions of the American flag as possible. If you can't find actual flags of earlier design, use red, white, and blue bunting and pictures of early flags.

Favors/Prizes: The give-aways are, you guessed it, flags. A small American flag for each guest is a must, as well as larger flags as prizes in games.

Games/Activities: Give the children a brief lesson on the history and evolution of the flag. Have lots of red, white, and blue paper on hand and let them construct their early American flags. Hang the flags on the wall until the party is over, when each child can take his or hers home.

Food: Just plain all-American food, like hot dogs and soda.

Costumes: Try to avoid excessive expense or effort. Dressing up as early American patriots can be fun and relatively easy. (Just make sure that all the girls don't come as Betsy Ross, and all the boys as George Washington.)

Groundhog Day

Invitations: Type up and copy an invitation that incorporates the legend of Groundhog Day.

Decorations: Decorate one room, or one side of a large room, for winter, with winter sports gear, skiing posters, and so on. Decorate the other side of the room for summer, with summer sports gear, surfing posters, and beach scenes.

Favors/Prizes: Give away the winter and summer scene posters at the end of the party.

Games/Activities: Play "Hide-and-Seek," preferably out in the woods. Have a treasure hunt by dividing the children into teams and have them follow hidden clues to find a toy stuffed groundhog (or something as close to it as you can find). Listen to radio station "on-the-scene" reports of groundhog sightings.

Food: Lots of "groundhog food"—nuts, granola bars, and fruit.

Costumes: Give the children the option of coming dressed in summer or winter clothing. Those that guessed correctly as to the groundhog's prediction win the prizes.

Halloween

Particularly for younger children, a Halloween party is a good way to cut down on the trick-or-treating, and to get them off the streets early.

Invitations: Cut letters out of newspapers or magazines and paste up a ransom-note-type invitation, warning of the consequences of not attending. Just make one note and photocopy it.

Decorations: You can't go wrong with the usual goblins and pumpkins. You might want to take things a step further and see how gory you can make things. Little touches like a bloody rubber hand sticking out of a drawer or noises from a supposedly empty room can add to the fun.

Favors/Prizes: Anything but more candy.

Games/Activities: Good Halloween activities could include "Hide-and-Seek" in a dark basement. If the party is actually on Halloween, have canisters ready for the children to go out and trick-or-treat for an hour for donations for a charitable cause. Bobbing for apples is an old Halloween tradition that many children may never have seen. Fill a large tub or a sink with water and float apples in it. Each child tries to get an apple by biting into it while it bobs on top of the water. Make sure to get small apples for younger children.

Top things off by renting a horror movie, such as one of the *Halloween* or *Friday the 13th* movies. Or go with one of the early monster classics, such as *Frankenstein* or *Dracula*.

Food: Forget it. The kids have already had enough (or will soon have enough) to make them sick. If you must, the traditional Halloween snack is donuts and apple cider.

Costumes: Yes—anything.

Hanukkah

Hanukkah is the Jewish Feast of Lights, celebrated during eight days in December, generally around Christmas time.

Invitations: Include traditional symbols such as the Star of David or the nine-branched menorah.

Decorations: Have a real menorah, as well as some cut-out menorahs. Draw on poster board, or cut out Stars of David. Use blue and white crepe paper and streamers to decorate.

Favors/Prizes: Traditional dreidels (tops), candy coins, candles, or menorahs.

Games/Activities: Card games are traditional during Hanukkah, as is a game of chance played with the dreidel. A dreidel is a four-sided top, with a letter of the Hebrew alphabet on each side. Each player puts a set amount of money into the kitty, and takes turns spinning the top. Depending on which letter comes up, you win or lose. Here's what happens when each of the four letters comes up:

N (nun)—You get nothing.

G (gimel)—You win everything.

H (he)—You take half of the kitty.

S (shin)—You pay in an amount equal to half the kitty.

Food: Traditional foods include potato latkes, knishes and challah.

Costumes: Traditional Jewish, or blue and white clothing.

Independence Day

Invitations: Make copies of the Declaration of Independence and write the invitations on the back, or just attach the invitations if the copies are good enough that the children would want to keep them.

Decorations: Red, white, and blue anything.

Favors/Prizes: If any kind of fireworks are legal in your area, you might want to give out some relatively safe varieties, such as sparklers. Have the children use them at the party under close supervision, rather than take them home unsupervised.

Games/Activities: Have the children design and make their own T-shirts with patriotic themes and colors. Have an inexpensive, plain white T-shirt for each guest, and have the children decorate them with crayons, markers, or iron-on patches. The shirts can also be finger-painted with fabric paints. The latter in particular is best done outside or in the garage.

Food: Hot dogs, hamburgers, ice cream, and apple pie.

Costumes: Anything in red, white, and blue is fine. Children may also want to dress up as famous Americans of the Revolutionary period, or just as any famous Americans.

Labor Day

A good theme party for this day is one at which the children to pretend that they have joined the workforce.

Invitations: Type up the invitations in the form of an inter-office memo, calling a meeting at your house at the appointed time and day, and giving directions in strict corporate language on appropriate dress for the occasion.

Decorations: Decorate in an office look, with graphs on the walls and business papers and publications on the tables.

Favors/Prizes: Office supplies, including pens, pencils, paper clips, and memo pads.

Games/Activities: Play word-search games, finding as many words as possible that can be made with the letters in "Labor Day" or "coffee break" or "expense account."

Play card games during the coffee break, choosing "Hearts," "Old Maid," or others, depending on the ages of the children.

Food: Have a coffee break with hot chocolate and donuts, or a business lunch with chicken salad sandwiches or salads and "iced tea" (apple juice).

Costumes: The children should dress up as what they want to be when they grow up.

Last Day of School

This is a good opportunity for a party with a theme such as a jail break, a World War II prison camp escape, or a vacation in some exotic spot.

Invitations: Write the invitation on a piece of lined school paper and fold it up like a note to be passed in class.

Decorations: Travel posters with beach and surfing scenes, or mountain scenes with views of summer sports such as golf, cycling, or rafting.

Favors/Prizes: Suntan lotion and sunglasses.

Games/Activities: Plan outdoor action games which involve capture and escape. These could include "Cops and Robbers," tag, and "Hide-and-Seek."

Finish up by showing a movie, such as *National Lampoon's Summer Vacation.*

Food: Lots of vacation junk food.

Costumes: Have each child dress for his or her favorite summer sport.

Memorial Day

Children aren't likely to appreciate the true meaning of Memorial Day, but they understand it's a holiday. Treat it as a "welcome to summer" holiday for younger kids.

Invitations: Use a summer theme—sunglasses, a tall cool drink, beach toys, etc.

Decorations: Summer things—beach toys, umbrellas.

Favors/Prizes: Sunglasses, beach toys.

Games/Activities: A number of the games in Chapter 3 can be adapted to this theme. Any ball games can use a beach ball, for instance.

Food: This is an all-American holiday, calling for traditional all-American food. Serve hot dogs and hamburgers, preferably from the grill. Add cole slaw, potato salad, and top it off with apple pie and ice cream.

Costumes: Summer vacation clothes!

New Year's Day

Since kids can't stay up late on New Year's Eve, and since parents were likely out having their own observance, New Year's Day can be their time to celebrate. Have a child-oriented New Year's Eve party.

Invitations: A page of the new January calendar. The New Year Baby coming in and Father Time heading out. A festive colorful rendition of the new year with streamers and confetti.

Decorations: Leave the decorations up from your New Year's Eve celebration. Plenty of balloons, streamers, confetti. Depending on how much you celebrated the night before, you might want to hide the noisemakers.

Favors/Prizes: Calendars, noisemakers.

Games/Activities: Do a trivia game about the year just ended. Find out important, happy events for each guest and include them in the game.

Food: Anything will do; have some sort of sparkling punch for a toast to the New Year.

Costumes: Party hats, sashes with the new year's date on them.

President's Day

How boring, you say. But wait, we're not talking about cherry pies and stovepipe hats here. We're talking about an excuse for a party! Why limit yourself to being president of some country? Why not be President of the Moon, or President of the Candy Store, or President of Videogames? Let your imagination go, and hail to the chief!

Invitations: Inauguration announcement with presidential seal.

Decorations: Make a variety of whimsical presidential seals on poster boards.

Favors/Prizes: Political-style buttons, ribbons, funny hats.

Games/Activities: Have each guest describe what they are "president of" and what their platform is.

Food: Food can be just about anything to follow the theme. Cherry pie, if you want a touch of tradition. Bull Burgers or Bologna sandwiches might be appropriate.

Costumes: It's certainly boring to dress up like the President of the United States, and dressing up as historical presidents leaves girls pretty much out of the game. So go with the imaginary presidents as described above. Either assign a "presidency" to each guest, or let him dream up his own.

St. Patrick's Day

Invitations: Cut shamrocks from green construction paper and hand letter the invitations on the back.

Decorations: Lot of shamrocks, either homemade or store-bought. String green streamers from the ceiling and hang a map of Ireland on the wall.

Favors/Prizes: Shamrocks or other lucky charms.

Games/Activities: Have a snake hunt. Hide rubber snakes around the yard, with each one redeemable for a prize.

Food: Make sugar cookies and ice them with green frosting.

Costumes: Just have everyone wear as much green as possible.

Thanksgiving

This would be a good opportunity for a history lesson about the founding of our country, and the basis of the Thanksgiving legend in the early American settlements. For avid football fans, Thanksgiving means football. If you are giving a party for older boys, forget about traditions and concentrate on football.

Invitations: Trace a picture of a turkey, or use a turkey-shaped cookie cutter, to produce turkey outlines on construction paper. Hand letter the invitations, and decorate them with feathers.

Decorations: Decorate the house, particularly the dinner table, with the traditional symbols of bounty, including dried ears of corn in the husk, pumpkins, and squash.

Favors/Prizes: Horns of plenty full of treats.

Games/Activities: "Turkey Hunt": this can be a treasure hunt or a scavenger hunt activity.

Food: The big decision: turkey or not turkey. If the party is actually on Thanksgiving Day and most of the children will be having dinner at home, the answer is: no turkey. If the party is a day or two after Thanksgiving, turkey sandwiches are okay.

Costumes: Try to keep it simple, but the children can have fun dressing up as Indians or early settlers.

Valentine's Day

Whether or not to have a Valentine's Day party depends a lot on the ages of the children. For very young children, it is just good fun and a chance to share friendships. As the children get older, some of them, particularly the boys, may feel that this kind of thing is too mushy. Older still, the children can be torn between having feelings and not wanting to express them, particularly in front of adults.

Invitations: The basic requirements are that they are red and white and have hearts on them. Buy some commercial invitations, or make your own.

Decorations: Same basics as for invitations. Hang red and white streamers from the ceiling and on the walls. Cut out red paper hearts of various sizes and hang them on the walls.

Favors/Prizes: Anything with the heart and red/white motif.

Games/Activities: Have lots of red and white construction paper, lace trim, and glue on hand, and let the children make Valentines for their parents or brothers and sisters.

A good game to play is "Broken Hearts." Before the guests arrive, cut heart outlines from red construction paper, making one for every two children who will be attending. Then cut each heart in half, making sure that you use bold, jagged, and unique cuts on each heart. Mix up the parts and hand them out at random to the children as they arrive. When everyone is ready, explain the game and give the signal to begin looking for the other half of the heart. The first two children to put their heart back together are the winners.

Food: Make a white cake (heart-shaped if you feel ambitious) and frost it with red icing. Heart-shaped sugar cookies can also be decorated with red frosting.

Costumes: Full costumes might be a bit too much, but it is fun to dress up in a lot of red and white colors, with heart accessories.

Recipes

The following pages contain the recipes mentioned in this book and some other basic recipes that you might need to prepare a successful selection of party foods.

These recipes are based, for the most part, on the greater economy of preparing all of the food from scratch, and assume at least limited cooking experience. As such, they are meant for the adults rather than the children. Older children should be able to make many of these recipes with adult supervision, however.

The recipes are presented in four main sections to cover major menu needs of the party:

- Beverages. If you don't want to serve soft drinks, this section presents a variety of fresh and healthy alternatives.
- Snacks. If you decide not to serve a meal at your party, you may still want to have some snacks available for the guests, or for their parents.
- Main course items. If you are serving a light meal, here are some ideas, including breakfast items for the morning after a slumber party or camp out.

- Desserts. Of course, desserts are the heart of a kids' birthday party. Included are basic cake recipes, icing recipes, and a wide selection of other treats, such as cookies, brownies, and candy.

Beverages

Assorted Beverages

apple juice
chocolate milk
hot chocolate
milk
orange juice

A&A Punch

1 qt. apple juice
2 cups apricot nectar
2 cups club soda
3 Tbsp. lemon juice

Mix all ingredients and serve over ice.

Ambrosia Smoothie

1 cup unflavored yogurt
½ cup peeled fresh or canned pineapple chunks
½ cup cracked ice
1 ripe banana, sliced
3 Tbsp. coconut cream (or ⅓ cup shredded sweetened coconut)

Whirl until smooth in blender. Makes two servings.

Apples and Oranges

1 cup applesauce
1 cup orange juice

Blend applesauce until smooth, blend in orange juice. Serve over ice.

Apple Ale

1 qt. apple juice
16 oz. club soda

Mix together and serve.

Apple Shake

2 8-oz. containers of plain yogurt
2 apples peeled, cored, and cut up
2 tsp. lemon juice
2 tsp. honey

Combine all ingredients in blender. Blend until apples are smooth.

Black Cow

8 oz. root beer
½ cup vanilla ice cream

Pour a little root beer into a glass, drop in the scoop of ice cream, fill the glass with root beer.

Bunch-a-Punch

6 oz. can frozen orange juice
6 oz. can frozen lemonade
6 oz. can frozen grape juice
2 qt. lemon-lime soda

In large punch bowl prepare frozen juice concentrates according to directions. Just before serving, add soda.

Cantaloupe Milk Shake

½ cup milk
2 Tbsp. lemon juice
1 Tbsp. honey
1 ripe cantaloupe

Blend well until a foamy head forms; serve over ice.

Dragon Juice

1 can pineapple juice (46 oz.)
2 sticks cinnamon
¼ tsp. grated nutmeg
¼ tsp. allspice

Combine all ingredients in a large pan and bring to a boil. Cover and simmer for 30 minutes.

Fresh Fruit Shakes

½ cup milk
¼ cup yogurt
1 Tbsp. honey or molasses
1 Tbsp. wheat germ or nutritional yeast
Fruit of choice:
  1 peach or orange
  ½ banana
  ½ cup melon
  ½ cup berries
Chopped nuts, optional

Blend until smooth. Add ice cubes while blending. Add chopped nuts if desired. Serve immediately.

Fruit Punch

½ cup lemon juice
1 cup orange juice
½ cup sugar, or more to taste
16 oz. ginger ale

Mix juices and sugar; stir until sugar is dissolved. Add ginger ale and serve over ice.

Lemonade

8 cups water
2 cups lemon juice
1 ⅓ cups sugar

Combine all ingredients and stir until sugar dissolves. Serve over ice.

Milk Shakes

1 pint ice cream (any flavor to suit your taste)
½ cup milk
flavorings (optional)

Put milk and ice cream in a blender; blend until smooth.
Add a little more milk if the shake is too thick.
Flavorings: Most of these flavorings work best with chocolate or vanilla ice cream, but let your own tastes be your guide. Add malted milk powder to make a malt. Other possible flavors to add are 2 Tbsp. of peanut butter, a favorite candy bar, or three or four favorite cookies.

Orange Nectar

½ cup fresh orange juice
2 soft bananas
3 Tbsp. honey
¼ tsp. almond extract
1 qt. milk

Blend until frothy and serve at once.

Orange Vanilla Cooler

1 cup vanilla ice cream
2 8-oz. containers of orange yogurt
2 cups cold orange juice

Mix all ingredients in a blender until smooth.

Strawberry Shake-Up

1 cup fresh strawberries
1 cup fresh orange juice
1 Tbsp. honey

Blend well and serve over ice.

Watermelon Crush

1 cup of ripe watermelon, pureed
½ cup fresh lemon juice
½ tsp. grated lemon rind
1 Tbsp. honey
2 cups water

Blend just until the honey is dissolved.

Yogurt Smoothie

1 ½ cups milk
1 8-oz. carton vanilla yogurt
1 Tbsp. powdered sugar
3 ice cubes
Choice of fruit:
  1 banana,
  2 peaches, or
  1 cup strawberries

Combine all ingredients in blender and blend until smooth; add ice cubes one at a time while blender is running.

Winter Toddy

2 cups apple cider
4 cloves, whole
2 cinnamon sticks
¼ tsp. allspice

Combine ingredients in saucepan and heat to just boiling. Strain into mugs to remove cinnamon sticks and cloves.

Zoo Milk

2 cups milk
½ cup peanut butter
1 banana

Blend all ingredients until smooth; serve.

Snacks

Assorted Snacks

Apple slices with peanut butter
Cheese cut into cubes, sticks, or shapes
Crackers, various shapes and flavors
Dried fruits, assorted (raisins, dates, others)
Fresh fruit, assorted, cut up
Fresh vegetables, cut up
Granola
Nuts and seeds
Trail mix

Bacon and Horseradish Dip

½ cup crisp-cooked bacon, crumbled
1 Tbsp. horseradish
8 oz. container of sour cream or plain yogurt
1 Tbsp. minced onion
1 Tbsp. minced parsley
6 oz. cream cheese, softened

Mash all ingredients together with a fork, then mix well. Chill before serving. Serve with assorted chips and crackers.

Bean Dip

2 cups cooked pinto beans (16-oz. can)
2 cloves garlic, crushed
½ cup onion, finely minced
½ tsp. salt
¼ tsp. cumin, ground
black pepper to taste
dash or more of Tabasco to taste

Mash beans and stir in all remaining ingredients. Serve hot or cold.

Dip Tips

ASSORTED DIPPERS
carrot sticks
celery sticks
corn chips
crackers
potato chips
tortilla chips
DIP BASES (choose one)
2 cups sour cream
2 cups low-fat cottage cheese, blended smooth in a food processor
2 pkgs. (6 oz.) cream cheese, beat with 3 Tbsp. plain yogurt until smooth
2 cups plain yogurt
DIP FLAVORINGS
avocado, 1 mashed with 1 tsp. lemon juice
bacon bits
chives, chopped
curry powder
garlic, crushed or powder, to taste
horseradish, 1 Tbsp. or more to taste
onion, grated, 2 Tbsp.
shrimp, cooked and chopped, ½ cup
Worcestershire sauce, 1 tsp.

Choose a dip base; mix in desired flavorings to taste. Cover and refrigerate about 1 hour to let flavors blend. Serve with a selection of dipping items.

Fried Cheese Sticks

8 oz. cheddar cheese
¾ cup finely crushed cornflakes
spices to taste (salt, pepper, garlic powder, cayenne)
2 eggs, beaten
oil for deep-fat frying
sauce for dipping (optional: use salsa or another dip)

Cut the cheese into sticks about 2 inches long, and ½ inch square.

Combine the crushed cornflakes and spices in a shallow pan.

Dip the cheese sticks into the beaten eggs, then roll in the cornflake mixture to completely coat the cheese. Repeat to get a thick coating.

Put the coated cheese sticks in the refrigerator for at least 2 hours.

Deep fry the sticks in 375°F oil a few at a time, for about 30 seconds, until they are golden. Drain on absorbent paper and serve.

Easy Nachos

½ bag of tortilla chips (10 oz.)
4 oz. processed cheese spread
½ cup chopped tomato
½ cup ripe olives, pitted and sliced

Warm the corn chips in a 250°F oven while heating the cheese spread over low heat in a small saucepan. Place chips on a serving platter, pour cheese over them, and top with tomato and olives. (Cheese can also be heated in a microwave for about 1 minute on high.)

Note: To make your own low-fat and low-salt tortilla chips, buy fresh tortillas (usually in the grocery's refrigerated section) and cut into 6 triangles. Place in a single layer on a cookie sheet, bake in a 400°F oven for 5 minutes. Turn chips over and bake 5 more minutes until crisp.

Magic Wands and Magic Dip

FOR THE DIP:
1 cup sour cream or yogurt
1 cup low-fat cottage cheese
1 envelope vegetable soup and dip mix
FOR DIPPING:
celery sticks cut into long "wands"
carrots cut into long "wands"
cucumbers cut into long "wands"

Combine all dip ingredients and blend until smooth. Chill at least two hours; serve with magic wands.

Party Pinwheels

3 oz. cream cheese, softened
5 slices bacon, cooked and crumbled
2 tsp. finely chopped onion
1 tsp. milk
8 oz. can refrigerated crescent dinner rolls
2 tsp. grated Parmesan cheese

Combine cheese, bacon, onion and milk and set aside. Separate the roll dough into 4 rectangles. Spread ¼ of cheese mixture on each rectangle, leaving a ¼-inch margin on one long side and no margin on the other sides. Roll dough jellyroll fashion, starting at long side with mixture spread to the edge. Pinch seam to seal. Cut each roll into 8 round pieces; place on greased cookie sheet. Sprinkle with Parmesan cheese and bake at 375°F for 10–12 minutes until lightly brown. Makes 32 pieces.

Quesadillas

1 pound of cheese, shredded (Cheddar, Jack or combination)
12 flour tortillas
choice of toppings
salsa
sour cream

Spread about ½ cup of cheese on a tortilla, put on desired toppings, and bake on a cookie sheet in a 450°F oven about 5 minutes until cheese is melted. Fold the tortilla in half and serve. To serve as appetizers, fold the tortilla in half, then cut into wedges. Serve with salsa and sour cream.

Quesadilla Toppings: chopped green onions, jalapeño peppers, bell peppers, beans, nuts, chopped olives, chopped onion, sunflower seeds, chopped tomato.

Salsa

4 large tomatoes
½ cup onion, finely chopped
¼ cup green pepper, finely chopped
¼ cup cilantro, finely chopped
2 cloves garlic, crushed
1 tsp. jalapeño pepper, minced
1 Tbsp. olive oil
2 tsp. lemon juice
dash of Tabasco
salt and pepper to taste

Cut tomatoes in half and remove seeds, then chop finely. Combine chopped tomatoes and all other ingredients in a bowl, mix well and let the flavors blend for an hour or so. Serve with tortilla chips.

Vegetable Ranch Dip

2 eight-oz. containers sour cream or plain yogurt
⅓ cup ketchup
½ tsp. Worcestershire sauce
1 envelope dry ranch-style salad dressing mix
½ tsp. instant minced onion
⅛ tsp. garlic salt
Tabasco sauce to taste

Combine all ingredients; blend well. Chill at least one hour.

Main Course Items

Bean and Cheese Burritos

8 flour tortillas
1 cup onion, chopped
1 Tbsp. oil
16 oz. refried beans
1 ½ cups cheese, grated (cheddar or jack)

Wrap tortillas in foil and heat for 10 minutes in 350°F oven.

Heat the oil in a heavy skillet and cook the onion until tender. Add the beans, cooking and stirring until they are hot. Spread about ¼ cup of beans on each tortilla; add some cheese, and roll the tortilla up. Serve with salsa.

Buttermilk Pancakes

1 cup all-purpose flour
2 Tbsp. sugar
1 tsp. baking powder
½ tsp. baking soda
1 cup buttermilk
1 Tbsp. vegetable oil
1 egg, slightly beaten

Combine first four ingredients and stir together well. Combine other ingredients and stir into dry ingredients until just smooth. Spoon in ¼-cup portions onto a hot griddle, turning when the tops are covered with bubbles and the edges have cooked. Makes 8 pancakes.

Challah

1 pkg. dry yeast
1 cup warm water
4 cups flour (unsifted)
⅓ cup sugar
1 tsp. salt
½ cup vegetable oil
3 eggs
poppy seeds (optional)

Mix the yeast in the warm (not hot) water until dissolved. Set aside.

Lightly beat the eggs until just combined, then set aside 2 Tbsp. to use later as a glaze.

Combine the flour, sugar, and salt in a large bowl. Make a well in the center of this flour mixture, and pour in the yeast mixture, the eggs, and the oil. Mix together, then knead the dough until it is smooth and elastic. Add more flour if it is too sticky.

Let the dough rise in a warm place until it doubles in size. Punch it down and knead slightly. Divide the dough into 3 equal parts, and roll each into a long rope of equal thickness. Braid together, place on greased, floured baking sheet. Cover and let rise until almost double in size. Brush with reserved egg.

Bake in preheated 400°F oven for 15 minutes; reduce heat to 375°F and bake about 45 minutes more.

French Toast

1 egg
¼ cup milk
1 tsp. vanilla
½ tsp. cinnamon

Lightly beat egg and beat in other ingredients. Dip slices of bread (preferably day-old) into mixture on both sides; brown both sides on hot buttered skillet.

Gingerbread Pancakes

1 cup flour, all-purpose
1 ½ tsp. baking powder
½ tsp. cinnamon
½ tsp. ginger
1 dash cloves, ground
½ cup skim milk
3 Tbsp. molasses
1 Tbsp. vegetable oil
1 egg, slightly beaten

Combine first five ingredients and stir well in a large bowl. Combine remaining ingredients, add to dry ingredients, and stir until smooth.

Pour in ¼-cup portions onto a hot griddle, turning when bubbles appear on the top and the edges are cooked.

No-Meat Chili

2 ½ cups black beans, uncooked
1 cup brown rice, uncooked
4 cloves garlic, minced
2 cups onion, chopped
2 cups green pepper, chopped
2 cups tomatoes, chopped
2 Tbsp. lemon juice
2 tsp. cumin, ground
3 tsp. chili powder
6 oz. tomato paste
½ tsp. cayenne
½ tsp. Tabasco
3 Tbsp. olive oil

Boil the beans in plenty of water with a little baking soda, and let stand one hour. Drain, then cook in a large, heavy pot in 6 cups of lightly salted water. Add enough water to keep the beans covered if it boils off.

After about an hour, stir in the brown rice, and continue cooking until rice is tender.

Meanwhile, cook the onion and garlic in the olive oil in a heavy skillet. When the onions are clear and tender, but not brown, add the spices and green pepper. Cook until pepper is tender.

Stir the tomato paste into the bean mixture, adding a little more water if needed. Add tomatoes and onion-pepper-spice mixture. Combine and cook slowly.

Serve topped with cheese if desired.

Pizza Dough

1 package dried yeast
1 Tbsp. sugar
1 cup warm water
3 cups flour
¼ tsp. salt
olive oil

Combine the yeast, sugar, and water in a large bowl. Mix, and let stand for 5 minutes.

Stir in all but ¼ cup of the flour, the salt, and oil. Mix until a soft dough forms. Turn the dough out onto a floured surface and knead until smooth and elastic, adding the remaining flour as needed a little at a time to keep dough from sticking.

Put dough into an oiled bowl, and turn to coat all over with the oil. Cover and let stand in a warm place for about 45 minutes.

When ready to use, punch the dough down, divide in half, and roll on a floured surface into 12-inch rounds. Place on pizza pan, top with sauce and toppings. Bake at 425°F for about 20 minutes, until edges are golden.

Makes two 12-inch pizzas

Pizza Dough (Food-Processor)

1 ⅓ cups warm water
1 package dried yeast
1 tsp. sugar
½ tsp. salt
2 Tbsp. olive oil
3 ½ cups flour
flour for kneading
olive oil for the bowl

Set up the food processor with the sharp blade. Pour in the water, sprinkle the yeast into it, and let it stand for 5 minutes.

Add the sugar, salt, oil, and ½ cup of flour. Run the processor until these ingredients are just combined.

With the motor running, gradually add the remaining flour through the feed tube, and run the processor until, and about a minute after, the dough forms a ball on top of the blade.

Put the dough on a floured board, form it into a ball, then put it in an oiled bowl, turning to cover with oil all over. Cover and leave the dough in a warm place for 45 minutes. When ready to use, punch the dough down, divide in half, and roll on a floured board to a 12-inch round. Transfer the round to a pizza pan, top as desired, and bake at 425°F for about 20 minutes, or until the edges are golden.

Makes two 12-inch pizzas

Pizza Dough, Whole Wheat

1 package dried yeast
1 Tbsp. honey
1 cup warm water
2 cups whole wheat flour
1 cup all-purpose flour
¼ tsp. salt
olive oil

Dissolve yeast and honey in a large bowl with the warm water. Let stand for about 5 minutes.

Stir in all but ¼ cup of the whole wheat flour, the all-purpose flour, salt, and oil. Mix until a soft dough forms. Turn the dough out onto a floured surface and knead until smooth and elastic, adding the remaining flour as needed a little at a time to keep dough from sticking.

Put dough into an oiled bowl, and turn to coat all over with the oil. Cover and let stand in a warm place for about 45 minutes.

When ready to use, punch the dough down, divide in half, and roll on a floured surface into 12-inch rounds. Place on pizza pan, top with sauce and toppings. Bake at 425°F for about 20 minutes, until edges are golden.

Makes two 12-inch pizzas

Pizza Sauce

4 oz. tomato sauce
1 Tbsp. oregano
1 tsp. garlic powder
salt to taste
pepper to taste

Mix spices into tomato sauce. Spread on pizza.

Pizza Toppings

black olives, chopped
browned ground beef
Canadian bacon, thinly sliced
green pepper, chopped or thinly sliced
Italian sausage, crumbled and browned
mozzarella cheese, grated
mushrooms, sliced
onions, chopped or thinly sliced
Parmesan cheese, grated
pepperoni, thinly sliced
Romano cheese, grated
tomatoes, chopped or thinly sliced

Add any combination of these to pizza dough which has been spread with pizza sauce.

Potato Latkes

4 potatoes, coarsely grated
½ cup onion, grated or very finely chopped
1 egg, lightly beaten
½ tsp. salt
pepper to taste
2 Tbsp. flour
vegetable oil for frying
    TOPPING:
8 oz. sour cream
¼ tsp. cinnamon (optional)
¼ tsp. sugar (optional)

Combine the grated potatoes and onion. Let stand for a few minutes and drain off any excess liquid. Add egg, salt, and pepper. Add flour, and a bit additional if needed to absorb excess moisture. The mixture should not be watery.

Heat oil ¼-inch deep in a heavy skillet until very hot. Drop the latke mixture by tablespoon into the hot oil. Fry until brown on both sides. Drain and serve topped with sour cream. Mix cinnamon and sugar into the sour cream if desired.

Pumpkin Pancakes

1 cup flour, all-purpose
2 Tbsp. brown sugar
2 Tbsp. baking powder
½ tsp. pumpkin pie spice
1 cup milk, skim
½ cup pumpkin, cooked and mashed
1 Tbsp. vegetable oil
2 egg whites

Combine the first four ingredients in a large bowl and stir well. Combine milk, pumpkin, and oil, and add to dry ingredients, stirring until smooth. Beat egg whites at room temperature until stiff peaks form, then gently fold into the batter.

Pour ⅓ cup portions onto a hot griddle and turn when the tops are covered with bubbles and the edges are cooked.

Quiche

1 pie crust (buy or make one)
½ cup chopped onion
1 Tbsp. oil
½ pound Swiss cheese, grated
3 eggs
1 ½ cups cream
½ tsp. salt
½ tsp. dry mustard
¼ tsp. nutmeg
pepper to taste

Bake the crust for 5 minutes at 375°F. Sauté the onion in the oil.

Beat the eggs, then beat in the cream and seasonings.

Spread the grated cheese over the bottom of the pie crust, top with the onion, then pour in the egg mixture.

Bake at 375°F for about 40 minutes, until the center is set. Let cool for 10 minutes, then serve.

Note: You can add other fillings at the same time as the onion. Good choices are sauteed mushrooms, green pepper, black olives, seafood, or sausage.

Quiche Pie Crust

1 ½ cups flour
¼ tsp. salt
½ cup shortening
3–4 Tbsp. cold water

Mix the flour and salt in a bowl, and cut the shortening into the flour, using a pastry blender, until the mixture looks like bread crumbs.

Add the water a tablespoon at a time, stirring and adding water just until the dough holds together.

Roll the dough out on a floured surface until it is about 2 inches larger than your pie pan. Transfer the dough to the pan. Makes one 9-inch crust.

Snakes on Buns

hot dogs
hot dog rolls
mustard
carrots cut into matchstick size (optional)

Make five or six cuts into the first half of the hot dog, about ½-inch deep and ½-inch apart. Turn the hot dog over, and repeat on the second half on the opposite side. Drop into boiling water to cook. In about 5 minutes they will be done and curled up into snake shapes.

Add dots of mustard for eyes, and optional carrot piece for a tongue. Serve on hot dog roll.

Tacos

12 taco shells
1 pound ground meat (beef or pork)
½ cup onion, chopped
2 cloves garlic, pressed or minced
1 jalapeño pepper, finely chopped
2 tsp. chili powder
   dash Tabasco
½ head iceberg lettuce, shredded
1 tomato, chopped
1 cup cheese (cheddar or jack), shredded

Cook meat, onion, and garlic in a heavy skillet until the meat is cooked through. Drain excess fat, then stir in pepper and spices. Simmer while you heat taco shells.

Fill each taco shell with meat mixture, then top with lettuce, tomatoes, and cheese.

Desserts

Cakes

Chocolate Cake

2 cups sifted flour
1 ½ cups sugar
⅓ cup cocoa, unsweetened
¼ tsp. baking soda
1 ½ tsp. baking soda
½ tsp. salt
1 cup milk
⅔ cup butter or margarine
1 tsp. vanilla
2 eggs, lightly beaten

Preheat oven to 350°F grease and flour two 8-inch pans or one 13 x 9 x 2 -inch pan.

Mix soda, baking powder, salt and cocoa with flour, and sift together. Cream the butter and sugar together, then beat the eggs in until smooth. Mix in vanilla, then slowly mix in flour and milk, adding some flour, then some milk. Pour batter into prepared pans and bake 25 or 30 minutes until done.

"Dirt" Cake

8 oz. cream cheese
1 cup powdered sugar
¼ cup butter
2 pkgs. vanilla pudding
2 ⅔ cup milk
1 large container whipped topping
1 large pkg. Oreo cookies
"gummy worms"
1 medium flowerpot
1 shovel

Combine cream cheese, sugar, and butter. Mix pudding and milk. Combine cheese mixture and pudding. Fold in whipped topping. Crumb cookies in food processor until all white disappears. Place piece of foil in bottom of clean flower pot. Layer crumbs and mixture three times until you reach the top of container. Place some "gummy worms" in layers and 3 on top of cake. Add some flowers, flags, etc. Place a garden spade in pot for serving. End with "dirt" on top (Oreo crumbs).

Another "Dirt" Cake

1 large pkg. instant vanilla pudding
1 large container whipped topping
1 pkg. cream cheese (8 oz.)
1 ¼ lb. Oreo cookies, crumbled
1 tsp. vanilla
1 tsp. lemon juice
"gummy worms"
1 medium flowerpot
1 shovel

Mix pudding according to directions. Add cream cheese, whipped topping, vanilla, and lemon juice to pudding and beat slow until well mixed. Starting with layer of crumbled cookies on bottom of pot, alternate layers of cookie and pudding mix. Finish with layer of crumbled cookies. Add a few "gummy worms" and artificial flowers for a finishing touch.

Red Cake

½ cup margarine or butter
1 ½ cup sugar
2 eggs
2 Tbsp. cocoa
2 oz. red food coloring
1 cup buttermilk
1 tsp. baking soda
1 Tbsp. cider vinegar
1 tsp. salt
2 ¼ cup sifted cake flour
1 tsp. vanilla

Cream margarine or butter until smooth and creamy; add eggs and beat until well mixed. Stir cocoa into food coloring; add to creamed mixture. Beat until color is well blended. In a small bowl, combine buttermilk, baking soda, vinegar, and salt. Add to the cocoa mixture; beat 2 minutes. Add flour gradually, beating after each addition. Add vanilla. Pour into two well greased, floured 9″ cake pans. Bake at 350°F about 30 minutes, or until done. Cool slightly. Remove from pan to cooling rack and allow to cool completely. Frost with cream cheese or butter frosting.

White Cake

2 ¼ cups cake flour, sifted
2 ½ tsp. baking powder
¾ tsp. salt
¼ cup butter
¼ cup shortening
1 ⅓ cups sugar
2 tsp. vanilla
3 egg whites, unbeaten
1 cup milk

Preheat oven to 375°F. Grease and flour two 8-inch round pans or one 13″ x 9″ x 2″-inch pan.

Mix baking powder and salt into flour, sift together. Cream butter, shortening, and sugar together, beating until creamy. Mix in vanilla. Beat in egg whites. Now mix in flour and milk alternately in 3 or 4 small doses.

Pour batter into pan(s) and bake about 20 minutes until cake tests done.

Whole-Wheat Carrot Cake

1 cup sugar
1 cup brown sugar, packed
1 cup vegetable oil
1 tsp. vanilla
4 eggs
1 ½ cup whole-wheat flour
½ cup flour
1 tsp. baking soda
1 tsp. baking powder
1 tsp. salt
1 tsp. allspice
1 tsp. cinnamon
3 cups shredded carrots
1 cup walnuts, chopped

Heat oven to 350°F, grease and flour 13 x 9 x 2-inch pan.

Stir sugars, oil, vanilla, and eggs together in a large bowl, then beat about one minute. Stir in flours, baking soda and powder, salt, and spices. Stir in carrots and walnuts. Pour into pan and bake about 45 minutes until the center tests done.

Yellow Cake

3 cups flour, sifted
1 Tbsp. baking powder
2 cups sugar
1 ½ cups milk
½ cup butter or margarine, softened
2 tsp. vanilla
2 eggs

Preheat oven to 375°F. Grease and flour two 9-inch round baking pans, or one 13 x 9 x 2 -inch pan.

Sift flour and baking powder together, combine with sugar in a large bowl. Add milk, margarine, and vanilla, and beat until combined. Add eggs and beat until well combined. Pour into prepared pans and bake about 25 minutes, until the cake tests done.

Coffee Cakes

Becky's Coffee Cake

2 ½ cup flour
½ tsp. salt
½ tsp. soda
½ tsp. cinnamon
2 tsp. baking powder
½ tsp. nutmeg
2 cup brown sugar
⅔ cup shortening
1 cup buttermilk
2 eggs

Sift first 6 ingredients together, then cut in the brown sugar and shortening. Set aside 1 cup of this mixture for the topping.

Stir in the buttermilk and the slightly beaten eggs until the flour mixture is just moistened.

Pour into a greased 9-inch square pan. Sprinkle the reserved topping over the batter. Bake at 375°F about 40 minutes.

Quick Coffee Cake

¼ cup oil
1 egg, slightly beaten
½ cup buttermilk (or yogurt, or milk)
1 ½ cup all-purpose flour
¾ cup sugar
2 tsp. baking powder
½ tsp. salt
    TOPPING
¼ cup brown sugar
1 Tbsp. flour
1 tsp. cinnamon
1 Tbsp. butter, melted
½ cup walnuts, chopped (optional)

Combine the oil, egg, and milk. Mix the dry ingredients together and add to the milk mixture. Mix well, and pour into a greased 9 x 9 x 2 -inch pan.

Mix topping ingredients together and sprinkle over the batter. Bake in 375°F oven for 25 minutes.

Cupcakes

Chocolate Cupcakes

½ cup butter or margarine, softened
1 cup sugar
1 tsp. vanilla
4 eggs
1 ¼ cups unsifted all-purpose flour
¾ tsp. baking soda
1 ½ cups (16-oz. can) chocolate syrup

Cream butter, sugar, and vanilla in large mixer bowl until light and fluffy. Add eggs; beat well. Combine flour and baking soda; add alternately with syrup to creamed mixture. Fill paper-lined muffin cups (2 ½ inches in diameter) half full with batter. Bake at 375°F for 15 to 20 minutes, until cake tester comes out clean. Cool; frost as desired. About 2 ½ dozen cupcakes.

Icing/Frosting

Chocolate Frosting

⅓ cup butter or margarine
4 ½ cups confectioners' sugar, sifted
¼ cup milk
1 ½ tsp. milk
½ cup cocoa powder, unsweetened

Beat butter until fluffy. Gradually beat in ½ of the sugar, then the milk, cocoa, and vanilla. Beat in the rest of the sugar; add a little more milk if the frosting gets too thick.

Chocolate Cream Cheese Frosting

3 oz. cream cheese
¼ cup butter or margarine
1 tsp. vanilla
¼ cup cocoa powder, unsweetened
2 cups confectioners' sugar

Mix the cream cheese, butter, and vanilla. Beat together until soft, then beat in the cocoa powder and slowly beat in the sugar until the frosting reaches the right thickness. If it gets too thick, beat in a little milk.

Creamy Brownie Frosting

3 Tbsp. butter or margarine, softened
3 Tbsp. cocoa
1 Tbsp. light corn syrup or honey
½ tsp. vanilla
1 cup confectioners' sugar
1 to 2 Tbsp. milk

Cream butter, cocoa, corn syrup, and vanilla in a small mixer bowl. Add confectioners' sugar and milk; beat to spreading consistency.

Cream Cheese Frosting

3 oz. cream cheese
¼ cup butter
2 cups confectioners' sugar
1 tsp. vanilla

Work the cream cheese and milk together, beating until soft; slowly beat in the sugar, then the vanilla.

Decorating Icing

1 lb. confectioners' sugar
½ cup white shortening
6 Tbsp. milk
1 tsp. vanilla

Combine all ingredients and beat until very smooth. The icing should remain fairly stiff to be good for decorating use in a pastry bag. Divide into small portions and color with food coloring if desired.

Peanut Butter Frosting

⅓ cup creamy peanut butter
4 ½ cups confectioners' sugar
¼ cup milk
1 ½ tsp. vanilla

Beat the peanut butter until creamy, then beat in half the sugar, the milk, and the vanilla. Beat in the other half of the sugar, adding more milk if needed to make it softer.

White Icing

2 cups confectioners' sugar
¼ cup soft butter or margarine
¼ tsp. salt
1 tsp. vanilla
3 Tbsp. milk

Cream the sugar and butter together, add the other ingredients, and beat until smooth. Add more sugar to make icing thicker, more milk to make it thinner.

Candies

Microwave Peanut Brittle

1 cup sugar
½ cup water
½ cup light corn syrup
7 oz. dry roasted peanuts
¾ cup shredded coconut (optional)
1 tsp. vanilla
1 tsp. baking soda

Stir together sugar, water, and syrup in a 2-qt. casserole. Microwave on high (100%) for 12–14 minutes or until bubbly. Stir in nuts and microwave on high for another 4–6 minutes, or until light brown. Stir in coconut and vanilla and microwave on high for 1–2 minutes, or more, or until hard, cracking stage is reached. Add baking soda; stir until light and foamy. Pour mixture onto a lightly greased cookie sheet. Spread to ¼ -inch thickness. Cool and break into pieces. Makes 1 lb.

Rich Cocoa Fudge

3 cups sugar
⅔ cup cocoa
⅛ tsp. salt
1 ½ cups milk
¼ cup butter or margarine
1 tsp. vanilla

Butter 8- or 9-inch square pan; set aside. Combine sugar, cocoa, and salt in heavy 4-qt. saucepan; stir in milk. Cook over medium heat, stirring constantly, until mixture comes to full rolling boil. Boil, without stirring, to soft-ball stage, 234°F on a candy thermometer (or until syrup, when dropped into very cold water, forms a soft ball that flattens when removed from water). Bulb of candy thermometer should not rest on bottom of saucepan.

Remove from heat. Add butter and vanilla; do not stir. Cool at room temperature to 110°F (lukewarm). Beat until fudge thickens and loses some of its gloss. Quickly spread in prepared pan; cool. Cut into 1- to 1 ½ -inch squares. About 3 dozen candies.

Marshmallow-Nut Cocoa Fudge: Increase cocoa to ¾ cup. Cook fudge as directed. Add 1 cup marshmallow creme with butter and vanilla; do not stir. Cool to 110°F (lukewarm). Beat 10 minutes; stir in 1 cup broken nuts and pour into prepared pan. (Fudge does not set until poured into pan.)

Nutty Rich Cocoa Fudge: Beat cooked fudge as directed. Immediately stir in 1 cup chopped almonds, pecans or walnuts and quickly spread in prepared pan.

Cookies, Brownies and Bars

Best Brownies

½ cup butter or margarine, melted
1 cup sugar
1 tsp. vanilla
½ cup unsifted all-purpose flour
⅓ cup cocoa
¼ tsp. baking powder
¼ tsp. salt
½ cup chopped nuts
1 recipe's yield of Creamy Brownie Frosting (see page 215)

Blend butter, sugar, and vanilla in large bowl. Add eggs; using a wooden spoon beat well. Combine flour, cocoa, baking powder, and salt; gradually blend into egg mixture. Stir in nuts.

Spread in greased 9-inch square pan. Bake at 350°F for 20 to 25 minutes or until brownie begins to pull away from edges of pan. Cool; frost if desired.

Better Brownies

¾ cup butter
2 cups sugar
3 eggs
2 squares semisweet chocolate
4 squares unsweetened chocolate
1 tsp. vanilla
1 cup flour
1 ¼ cup chopped pecans

Melt the butter and margarine in a microwave, or in a heavy pan over low heat. Set aside to cool slightly. Beat eggs and sugar together until creamy. Mix all other ingredients into the egg and sugar mixture, then pour mixed batter into a greased 9 x 13-inch pan. Bake at 350°F for 30 minutes.

Brownie Cookies

4 oz. semisweet chocolate
1 oz. unsweetened chocolate
2 ⅓ cup sifted all-purpose flour
1 ½ tsp. baking soda
½ tsp. baking powder
¼ lb. unsalted butter
1 cup granulated sugar
1 Tbsp. vanilla extract
2 eggs
1 Tbsp. milk
¾ cup finely chopped walnuts

Melt the chocolate over hot water or in a microwave.

Sift the flour, baking soda, and baking powder together, then set aside.

Cream the butter in a mixing bowl, then slowly beat in the sugar. Add the vanilla, then beat in the eggs one at a time. Stir in the melted chocolate, then the flour mixture and the milk. When these ingredients are just mixed, stir in the walnuts.

Cover and refrigerate dough for 30 minutes before rolling. Meanwhile, preheat oven to 375°F and prepare a lightly greased cookie sheet.

Roll out the dough on a well-floured surface to a ¼ inch thickness and cut it into desired shapes. Re-roll scraps and cut again. Space the cut-out dough on the cookie sheet and bake for 6 minutes.

Brownies

4 squares chocolate, unsweetened
¾ cup butter
2 cups sugar
3 eggs
1 tsp. vanilla
1 cup flour, all-purpose
1 cup walnuts, chopped

Melt chocolate and butter in microwave or in a saucepan over very low heat, stirring constantly until just melted. Remove from heat.

Stir the sugar into melted chocolate until well blended, then mix in eggs and vanilla. Mix in flour, then the nuts. Spread mixture in a well-greased 13 x 9 inch pan. Bake at 350°F for 35 to 40 minutes, until wooden pick comes out clean. Cool in pan before serving. Makes 24 brownies.

Chocolate-Chip Cookies

1 cup (two sticks) butter, softened
¼ cup sugar
¾ cup brown sugar
2 eggs
1 tsp. vanilla
2 ¼ cups flour
1 tsp. salt
1 tsp. baking soda
1 cup walnuts, chopped
2 cups chocolate chips

Beat the butter until smooth, then beat in the sugars. When butter and sugar are well blended, beat in the eggs and vanilla until batter is fluffy. Sift the flour, salt, and soda together, then stir into the batter.

Stir in walnuts and chocolate chips.

Drop dough by heaping teaspoonfuls onto lightly greased cookie sheets. Bake at 375°F for about 10 minutes, until golden.

Cream Cheese Brownies

1 batch Brownie batter, ready to bake
　　CHEESE FILLING
6 oz. cream cheese
¼ cup sugar
1 egg
2 Tbsp. flour

Mix all cheese filling ingredients together, spoon over brownie batter in pan, and swirl with a knife to marbleize. Bake 40 minutes at 350°F.

Chocolate Almond Thins

1 cup butter
½ cup brown sugar
½ cup sugar
1 egg yolk
1 ½ tsp. vanilla
1 ¾ cup flour
1 cup almonds, chopped
1 cup semisweet chocolate pieces

Preheat oven to 350°F.

Cream together butter and both sugars. Beat in egg yolk and vanilla. Stir in the flour and half the almonds. Spread the mixture in ungreased 9 x 13-inch baking pan and bake for 20 minutes. Sprinkle hot crust with chocolate pieces, then with remaining almonds, pressing the nuts into the melting chocolate. Cut into squares while still warm, but don't remove from pan until cool.

Double Chocolate-Chip Cookies

1 ¾ cups white flour
¼ teaspoon baking soda
1 cup butter or margarine (softened)
1 tsp. vanilla extract
1 cup granulated sugar
½ cup dark brown sugar (firmly packed)
1 egg
⅓ cup unsweetened cocoa
2 Tbsp. milk
1 cup chopped pecans or walnuts
6 oz. (1 cup) semisweet chocolate chips

Combine flour and baking soda thoroughly and set aside. In the large bowl of an electric mixer, cream butter. Add vanilla and sugars and beat until fluffy. Beat in egg. At low speed, beat in cocoa and then milk. With a wooden spoon, mix in dry ingredients just until blended. Stir in nuts and chocolate chips. Drop by rounded teaspoonfuls onto nonstick or foil-lined baking sheets. Bake at 350°F for 12 to 13 minutes. Remove from oven and cool slightly before removing from baking sheets. Makes 3 dozen.

Old-Fashioned Chocolate-Chip Cookies

1 cup butter, softened
¾ cup sugar
¾ cup packed light brown sugar
1 tsp. vanilla
2 eggs
2 ¼ cups unsifted all-purpose flour
1 tsp. baking soda
½ tsp. salt
2 cups (12-oz. package) semisweet chocolate chips
1 cup chopped nuts (optional)

Cream butter, sugar, brown sugar, and vanilla in large mixing bowl until light and fluffy. Add eggs; beat well. Combine flour, baking soda, and salt; gradually add to creamed mixture. Beat well. Stir in chocolate chips and nuts.

Drop by teaspoonfuls onto ungreased cookie sheet. Bake at 375°F for 8 to 10 minutes or until lightly browned. Cool slightly. Remove from cookie sheet and cool completely on wire rack. About 6 dozen cookies.

Oatmeal Peanut-Butter Cookies

1 ½ cup flour
½ tsp. baking soda
1 tsp. cinnamon
½ tsp. salt
1 egg, lightly beaten
1 cup sugar
½ cup vegetable oil
½ cup melted margarine or butter
1 Tbsp. molasses
¼ cup milk
1 ¾ cup uncooked oatmeal
½ cup peanut butter (chunky style)
½ cup raisins (optional)
½ cup chopped nuts (optional)

Preheat oven to 350°F. Mix flour, soda, cinnamon, and salt together in a large bowl. Stir in remaining ingredients one at a time. Drop by teaspoonfuls on ungreased cookie sheet. Bake until edges are slightly brown, about 12 minutes. Makes about 6 dozen.

Oatmeal Shortbread

½ cup butter, unsalted, softened
⅓ cup brown sugar, firmly packed
¾ cup plus 2 Tbsp. all-purpose flour
½ tsp. salt
¾ tsp. cinnamon
¾ cup old-fashioned rolled oats

Preheat oven to 350°F.

Use an electric mixer to cream the butter in a large bowl; add the brown sugar, and beat the mixture until light and fluffy.

In another bowl mix together the flour, salt, and cinnamon. Add the flour mixture and the oats to the butter mixture and stir until just combined. Press into an ungreased 9-inch pie pan. Smooth the top and prick all over with a fork. Bake until golden, about 40 minutes. While still warm, score all the way through with a fork to form wedges. After completely cool, break into wedges and serve.

Peanut Butter Bars

1 cup crunchy peanut butter
⅔ cup butter or margarine, softened
1 tsp. vanilla
2 cups firmly packed brown sugar
3 eggs
1 cup sifted flour
½ tsp. salt
¾ cup powdered sugar
2 tsp. water
¼ cup semisweet chocolate chips
1 tsp. shortening

Combine first 3 ingredients in a large bowl and beat until well blended. Beat in sugar until light and fluffy; beat in eggs, one at a time. Stir in flour and salt just until well blended. Spread batter into a greased 3 x 13 -inch pan and bake for 35 minutes at 350°F. Cool slightly. Combine powdered sugar with water in a small bowl. Stir until smooth, spread over still-warm cookies in pan. Melt chocolate chips and shortening together. Drizzle from spoon over icing. When cool, cut into 36 rectangles and lift out carefully.

Peanut Butter Bites

½ cup sugar
½ cup light corn syrup
1 cup peanut butter
2 cups crispy rice cereal

Combine sugar and syrup in saucepan. Cook over medium heat until mixture comes to a boil, stirring constantly. Remove from heat; add peanut butter, stirring until mixture is smooth. Stir in cereal. Drop mixture by tablespoonfuls onto wax paper; let cool completely. Makes about 3 dozen.

Peanut Butter Cookies

1 cup butter (2 sticks)
1 cup sugar
1 cup brown sugar
2 eggs, beaten
1 cup peanut butter
3 cups flour
2 tsp. baking soda
¼ tsp. salt

Beat butter until creamy, then beat in the sugars until well blended. Beat in eggs until the batter is smooth, then mix the peanut butter in well.

Sift the flour, baking soda, and salt together, then stir until the dough is well mixed.

Roll the dough into small balls and place about an inch apart on ungreased cookie sheets. Press the balls of dough down with a fork twice to make a crosshatch pattern on the top.

Bake in a 350°F oven for about 10 minutes.

Peanut Butter Brownies

½ cup butter or margarine, softened
¼ cup peanut butter
1 cup sugar
1 cup packed light brown sugar
3 eggs
1 tsp. vanilla
2 cups unsifted all-purpose flour
¼ tsp. salt
½ cup (5.5-oz. can) chocolate syrup

Blend butter and peanut butter in large mixer bowl. Add sugar and brown sugar; beat well. Add eggs, one at a time, beating well after each addition. Blend in vanilla. Combine flour, baking powder, and salt; add to peanut butter mixture.

Spread half the batter in greased 13 x 9-inch pan. Spoon syrup over top. Carefully spread with remaining batter. Swirl with spatula or knife for marbled effect. Bake at 350°F for 35 to 40 minutes or until lightly browned. Cool; cut into squares.

Zebra Brownies

BOTTOM LAYER
1 cup butter
2 cups sugar
1 cup cocoa
4 eggs
1 cup flour
1 tsp. vanilla
TOP LAYER
3 cups cream cheese
1 ½ cup sugar
5 eggs
1 ½ tsp. vanilla
½ cup flour

For bottom layer, cream together softened butter and sugar with electric mixer on high speed; add cocoa and eggs; mix well on low speed. Mix in flour and vanilla. Pour this mixture into a greased 9 x 13-inch pan.

For top layer, whip cream cheese and sugar together, add eggs and mix in. Then mix in vanilla and flour. Pour the cheese mixture onto the chocolate layer and lightly swirl with spatula to marbleize. Bake at 350°F for 45 to 55 minutes.

Note: An alternative assembly method is to alternate the chocolate and cheese mixtures in 3-inch strips on the bottom layer, then alternate again in the opposite order on the top layer, before swirling together to marbleize them.

Other Goodies

Reindeer Treats

1 cup chopped walnuts
1 cup raisins
1 cup chopped pitted dates
2 Tbsp. honey
colored sprinkles, ground walnuts, or graham cracker
   crumbs

In a food processor, grind walnuts and set aside. Place raisins, dates, and honey in the processor and pulse two or three times until ingredients are combined. Combine the fruit and the walnuts, then shape the mixture into 1-inch balls. Roll the balls in sprinkles, ground nuts, or graham cracker crumbs to coat them.

Brownie Pizza

BROWNIE LAYER:

4 unsweetened chocolate squares
¾ cup margarine or butter (1½ sticks)
2 cups sugar
4 eggs
1 tsp. vanilla
1 cup flour, all purpose
     TOPPING:
1 pkg. cream cheese (8 oz)
¼ cup sugar
1 egg
½ tsp. vanilla
assorted sliced fruit
2 squares semisweet chocolate

Heat oven to 350°F. Line 12 x ½-inch pizza pan with foil (to lift brownie from pan after baking); grease foil. Melt chocolate and margarine or butter together in a heavy pan over low heat, or in the microwave. Stir until chocolate is completely melted. Stir 2 cups of sugar into melted chocolate mixture. Mix in 4 eggs and 1 tsp. vanilla until well blended. Stir in flour. Spread in prepared pizza pan. Bake for 30 minutes.

Topping: Mix cream cheese, ¼ cup sugar, 1 egg, and ½ tsp. vanilla together until well blended. Pour over hot, baked brownie crust and bake 10 minutes longer, or until toothpick inserted into center comes out with fudgy crumbs. Be careful not to overbake. Cool in pan. Lift brownie pizza out of pan, peel off foil, and put on a serving plate. Arrange fruit slices over cream cheese layer. Drizzle with melted semisweet chocolate.

Orange Fun-Pops

6 oz. orange juice concentrate
6 oz. water
1 cup plain low-fat yogurt
1 tsp. vanilla

Blend all ingredients and pour into popsicle containers. Freeze several hours.

After the Party's Over

Winding Down

Party plans should include a winding down process, to get the children settled down and ready to leave quietly. Serving the food is usually the signal of the end of the major activity. Plan the last activity to be something fairly sedate and noncompetitive. This would be a good time for a craft project, with each child producing something to take home. This is also the best time to distribute any party favors.

For a birthday party, you may want to arrange to have one child stay later than the rest, perhaps even overnight, to play quietly with your birthday child.

Continue to treat your child as the guest of honor after the others have gone. You and your other recruited helpers can handle the cleanup.

Make some private time to let the child know that you really think he or she is special, and that the gifts and party are only a small physical sign of that feeling.

Thank-You Notes

Teach your child to send a thank-you note for presents as soon as he or she is old enough to do so. Some children may want to make thank-you telephone calls instead of notes.

Adult relatives, especially Grandma and Grandpa, should definitely get a note or call. A nice touch is to send a snapshot of the birthday child with the gift received.

Cleaning Up

Your primary goals following a party for children are to clean up any spills or stains as quickly as possible, soak or rinse off any pots or pans that have caked-on food, get everything into the dishwasher, and ignore everything until the next day. Major cleaning is best left for a fresh start another time.

The major party clean-up problems are spills, spots, and stains on clothing, carpets, and furniture. Two key steps to effective stain removal are fast action and determining what caused the spot or stain. These are usually fairly easily accomplished at a children's party with close supervision.

The first step in cleaning up any spill is to remove the spilled material. This means getting it off, not rubbing it in. For solid spills, scrape up as much of the spilled matter as possible, using a dull knife and taking care not to harm the fabric or material. For liquids, blot up or sponge as much of the spill as possible, as soon as possible. The primary first aid treatment for potential stains is cold water. Except for a few delicate fabrics, such as silk, when in doubt, flush the spill with plain, cold water as soon as possible, and then do your research for particular care.

Fabrics

Different types of fabric require different treatment, even if they all claim to be washable. For clothing, the first step is the read the label in the garment. Follow any specific care instructions. If there are none, follow the directions below for the particular type of fabric. Unless instructed otherwise, below or on garment labels, remove particularly heavy stains by soaking in plain, cold water before laundering. Remember that heat will permanently set many stains, such as blood. Similarly, soap can set other stains, such as coffee or fruit. If in doubt, wash in cold water. Check to make sure that the stain is completely gone before putting the garment in the dryer.

Cotton: White can be washed in hot water, with bleach if desired. Rinse well and spin dry. Colored cottons can be washed together. Wash in warm to cold water, adding salt to the water to keep the colors from running.

Linen: White linen, such as sheets or napkins, can be washed like cotton. Colored linen should be washed in cool water without bleach. Squeeze the fabric as little as possible, and iron while slightly damp.

Satin: Satin should be hand-washed in warm soapy water, adding two tablespoons of kerosene per gallon of water. Do not squeeze or wring out the fabric. Rinse in warm water with a little borax in the final rinse to restore the finish. Gently squeeze out the water, and iron while still damp.

Silk: Very few silk garments are washable. Check the label, and then dry clean it anyway. To remove water spots from silk, let it dry and then rub the spot with another part of the garment.

Stuffed Toys: Remove any accessories and prespot any stains. Put the toy, together with any others that need cleaning, in a mesh laundry bag or a pillow case. Tie the end shut and wash in the gentle cycle.

Wool: Avoid water that is either very hot or very cold. Hand wash unless the garment label says that it is machine washable. Fine woolens should be washed in warm water with pure soap flakes. Agitate gently, avoiding wringing or twisting the garment, and rinse well. As an alternative, use a cold-water product specifically designed for wool, following the package directions.

Wool Blankets: Wool blankets can be machine washed, but they should not be agitated. This is what causes shrinking. Fill the machine, add detergent, and let it agitate enough to dissolve the detergent. Turn the machine off and put in the blanket. Let the blanket soak for fifteen minutes, and turn the machine control to the first spin cycle. Let the machine spin and fill with rinse water, and then turn it off again. Let the blanket soak in the rinse water for about five minutes, and turn the dial back to the spin cycle. Repeat the soaking, let the machine spin dry, and remove the blanket. Do not tumble dry.

Stains

Different types of stains require different treatments. At a child's party, your stains will be limited to a few common types (you won't have to worry about wine or coffee stains), and you will almost always know immediately what the stain is.

Berry Juice: Scrape off as much of the spill as possible, as quickly as possible, with a dull knife. Sponge off with cool water, repeating until no more color comes out. Rub the spot with a cut lemon or with lemon juice. Rinse with cool water, blot the spot dry with a clean white cloth, and let it air dry. When the garment is fully dry, apply laundry prewash, wash in warm water, and air dry.

Blood: Soak blood-stained garments in cool water until the stain turns a light brown. Remove any lingering traces from white garments with bleach, from colors with hydrogen peroxide. Wash as usual for the type of fabric.

Ketchup: Scrape off as much of the spill as possible with a dull knife, and then sponge off with cold water. Apply a laundry prewash and rinse. If any of the stain remains, sponge with a mixture of equal parts water and vinegar. Reapply prewash and wash in warm water.

Chocolate: Sponge off chocolate stains with cold water. The add two tablespoons of borax to two cups of water and sponge off the stain again. Rinse thoroughly and wash normally.

Felt-Tip Marker Ink: Check the marker to see if the ink is washable or permanent. If it is washable, sponge the stain with cleaning solvent until no more color comes out. Apply laundry prewash and a few drops of ammonia to the stain, and wash in warm water. If the ink is permanent, you will probably not be able to get it out. Rub the spot with insect repellent containing DEET, and rinse thoroughly. If that doesn't work, sponge the area with rubbing alcohol, repeating as needed. As a last resort, sponge with hydrogen peroxide.

Fruit: For stains from red fruit such as cherries or berries, see the entry on berry juice above. For others, such as apple or orange stains, blot up what you can with a clean cloth and sponge off with cool water immediately. Apply prewash to the stain and wash as usual.

Glue (Organic): Organic glues are water soluble, including white glue and paste. Scrape off as much as you can with a dull knife, taking care not to spread the glue any more. Sponge off with cool water, followed by a sponging with soap and water. Rinse well with cool water. Apply laundry prewash and wash in warm water.

Glue (Synthetic): Synthetic glues include most clear glues and cements. Scrape off as much as possible with a dull knife, taking care not to spread the glue around any more. Sponge off with cool water, and then with soap and water. If that doesn't work, try using a cleaning solvent. You may need acetone for plastic cement, but don't use it on acetates. Apply prewash and wash in warm water.

Grass Stains: Sponge off stains with rubbing alcohol before washing. It is best if the garment can be washed in hot water.

Grease: To remove grease or oil from clothes, blot up as much as you can without rubbing. Apply an absorbent such as kitty litter, and let it soak up the grease. Apply a laundry prewash and wash in hot water if possible. For old stains, apply petroleum jelly instead of using the absorbent, letting it stand for fifteen minutes.

Greasy Food Stains: For greasy food stains such as butter, margarine, or mayonnaise, scrape off as much as possible with a dull knife. Apply an absorbent such as cornmeal and let stand for several hours. Brush off, apply a laundry prewash, wash in warm water, and air dry.

Gum: Freeze the gum by rubbing it with ice. Then break it up and remove it. Rub garment spots with egg white before washing.

Jelly: Remove as much of a jelly, jam, or fruit syrup stain as possible by scraping with a dull knife. Sponge off with warm water. Apply a laundry prewash, sponge thoroughly with water, apply more prewash, and wash in warm water.

Ice Cream: If the ice cream is chocolate, see the specific directions for chocolate on page 239. For other flavors, sponge off with cool water, or with a detergent solution if possible. Apply laundry prewash, wash in warm water, and air dry.

Ink: Apply hair spray to the stain until damp and blot with a clean cloth. If the garment is polyester, try rubbing alcohol.

Milk: Remove milk stains by soaking the garment in cool water. Treat the spot with undiluted liquid detergent or a laundry prewash, and wash in warm water.

Mustard: Treat the spot with undiluted liquid detergent and then wash. If any stain remains, use diluted bleach on whites, hydrogen peroxide on colors.

Tomato Sauce: Scrape off as much as possible with a dull knife and sponge off with cold water. Apply laundry prewash and rinse. If the stain remains, sponge off with a solution of equal parts water and vinegar. Reapply the laundry prewash and wash in warm water.

Vomit: Scrape off as much as possible with a dull knife and flush well with cool water. Soak the garment in warm water, adding one tablespoon of detergent and two tablespoons of ammonia per quart of water. Rinse in cold water and wash normally.

Wax: If possible, freeze the garment, shatter the wax with a knife handle, and scrape off as much as possible. Put white paper towels on both sides of the stain and iron with a warm iron. Repeat with clean paper towels until all the wax is blotted out. Apply laundry prewash and wash, using hot water if possible.

Appendix:
Birthday Signs,
Symbols, Gifts

Birthstones & Flowers

Month	Gem	Flower
January	Garnet	Carnation/Snowdrop
February	Amethyst	Primrose
March	Aquamarine	Violet
April	Diamond	Daisy
May	Emerald	Hawthorn
June	Pearl	Rose
July	Ruby	Water lily
August	Peridot	Poppy
September	Sapphire	Morning glory
October	Opal	Calendula/Marigold
November	Topaz	Chrysanthemum
December	Turquoise	Poinsettia/Holly

Zodiac Birthsigns

January 20–February 19: Aquarius, The Water Bearer
Generous, popular, friendly, idealistic, refined, original, faithful, artistic, lucky, unselfish.

February 20–March 20: Pisces, the Fish
Gentle, kind, sympathetic, shy, emotional, honorable, sensitive.

March 21–April 19: Aries, the Ram
Brave, bold, noble, impulsive, intellectual, confident, independent.

April 20–May 20: Taurus, the Bull
Strong values, common sense, determined, devoted, gentle.

May 21–June 20: Gemini, the Twins
Like variety and doing more than one thing at once, easily bored, curious, sophisticated, ambitious, intelligent.

June 21–July 22: Cancer, the Crab
Nurturing, sensitive, romantic, sympathetic, imaginative, tenacious, curious.

July 23–August 22: Leo, the Lion
Warm, affectionate, generous, noble, creative, adventurous, temperamental.

August 23–September 22: Virgo, the Virgin
Demure, artistic, healer, kind, sympathetic, methodical.

September 23–October 23: Libra, the Scales
Attractive, sociable, artistic, perceptive, intuitive, orderly, sympathetic.

October 24–November 22: Scorpio, the Scorpion
Intense, determined, secretive, energetic, loyal, philosophical.

November 23–December 21: Sagittarius, the Archer
Practical, mature, imaginative, funny, fun-loving, loyal, independent, active.

December 22–January 19: Capricorn, the Goat
Ambitious, youthful, practical, economical, eager, ambitious.

Chinese Zodiac Birthsigns

The Chinese use a different zodiac system, with birth signs represented by different animals. Here are signs for kids (and their curious parents!).

Birth Year	Sign
1944	Monkey
1945	Rooster
1946	Dog
1947	Boar
1948	Rat
1949	Ox
1950	Tiger
1951	Rabbit
1952	Dragon
1953	Snake
1954	Horse
1955	Sheep
1956	Monkey
1957	Rooster
1958	Dog
1959	Boar
1960	Rat
1961	Ox
1962	Tiger
1963	Rabbit

1964	Dragon
1965	Snake
1966	Horse
1967	Sheep
1968	Monkey
1969	Rooster
1970	Dog
1971	Boar
1972	Rat
1973	Ox
1974	Tiger
1975	Rabbit
1976	Dragon
1977	Snake
1978	Horse
1979	Sheep
1980	Monkey
1981	Rooster
1982	Dog
1983	Boar
1984	Rat
1985	Ox
1986	Tiger
1987	Rabbit
1988	Dragon
1989	Snake
1990	Horse
1991	Sheep
1992	Monkey
1993	Rooster
1994	Dog
1995	Boar

Animal Sign Characteristics

The Year of the Rat: Cool, social, energetic, ambitious, practical, frugal.

The Year of the Ox: Gentle, patient, dependable, calm, independent, conscientious, logical, reliable.

The Year of the Tiger: Reckless, sincere, affectionate, generous, quick-tempered, charming, optimistic, verbal.

The Year of the Rabbit: Peaceful, sensitive, artistic, lucky, strong-willed, elegant.

The Year of the Dragon: Energetic, eccentric, successful, generous, active.

The Year of the Snake: Wise, charismatic, intelligent, suspicious.

The Year of the Horse: Cheerful, irresistible, independent, perceptive, versatile.

The Year of the Sheep: Gentle, compassionate, sensitive, romantic.

The Year of the Monkey: Risk-taker, quick-witted, charming, practical, shrewd.

The Year of the Rooster: Organized, precise, efficient, critical, combative.

The Year of the Dog: Loyal, kind, verbal, witty, amiable, appealing, strong.

The Year of the Boar: Honest, sturdy, easygoing, happy, well-adjusted, sincere, trustworthy, generous.

Gift Ideas

Backpacks

Beach towels

Bicycle

Board games

Books

Bulletin board

Camera
Caps
Cars and trucks
Cash
Computer accessories,
  software
Craft kits
Crayons and coloring books
Doctor kit
Doll
Doll accessories
Educational games
Electronic game
  accessories,
  cartridges
Gift certificate
Gloves
Hobby items
Jewelry
Jewelry box
Lego Blocks
Magazine subscription
Monogrammed clothing

Music recordings
  (records, tapes, CDs)
Pen and pencil set
Personal appliances
  (hair dryer, curling iron)
Play-Doh
Pocket calculator
Posters
Purses
Puzzles
Radio
Savings bonds
Slippers
Sports equipment
Stationery
Stuffed animal toys
T-shirts
Tape player
Tote bags
Umbrellas
Videotapes
Wagon
Watch

PARTY NOTES

PARTY NOTES

PARTY NOTES

PARTY NOTES

PARTY NOTES

Index

INFORMATIVE AND FUN READING

__THE ANIMAL RIGHTS HANDBOOK by Laura Fraser, Joshua
Horwitz, Stephen Tukel and Stephen Zawistowski
0-425-13762-7/$4.50

If you love animals and want the facts about how the fashion, food, and
product-testing industries exploit animals for profit, this book offers step-by-
step guidelines to save animals' lives in simple, everyday ways.

__THE RAINFOREST BOOK by Scott Lewis/Preface by Robert
Redford   0-425-13769-4/$3.99

Look into the spectacular world of tropical rainforests--their amazing
diversity, the threats to their survival, and the ways we can preserve them
for future generations. This easy-to-read handbook is full of practical tips
for turning your concern for rainforests into action.

__MOTHER NATURE'S GREATEST HITS by Bartleby Nash
0-425-13652-3/$4.50

Meet the animal kingdom's weirdest, wackiest, wildest creatures! Learn
about dancing badgers, beer-drinking raccoons, 180-foot worms, Good
Samaritan animals and more!

__FOR KIDS WHO LOVE ANIMALS by Linda Koebner with the
ASPCA   0-425-13632-9/$4.50

Where and how do animals live? How did they evolve? Why are they
endangered? Explore the wonders of the animal kingdom while you
discover how to make the Earth a safer home for all animals.

__SAFE FOOD by Michael F. Jacobson, Ph.D., Lisa Y. Lefferts and
Anne Witte Garland 0-425-13621-3/$4.99

This clear, helpful guide explains how you can avoid hidden hazards--and
shows that eating safely doesn't have to mean hassles, high prices, and
special trips to health food stores.

Payable in U.S. funds. No cash orders accepted. Postage & handling: $1.75 for one book, 75¢
for each additional. Maximum postage $5.50. Prices, postage and handling charges may
change without notice. Visa, Amex, MasterCard call 1-800-788-6262, ext. 1, refer to ad # 444

Or, check above books	Bill my:	☐ Visa	☐ MasterCard	☐ Amex	
and send this order form to:					(expires)
The Berkley Publishing Group	Card#				
390 Murray Hill Pkwy., Dept. B					($15 minimum)
East Rutherford, NJ 07073	Signature				
Please allow 6 weeks for delivery.	Or enclosed is my:	☐ check	☐ money order		
Name		Book Total	$		
Address		Postage & Handling	$		
City		Applicable Sales Tax	$		
		(NY, NJ, PA, CA, GST Can.)			
State/ZIP		Total Amount Due	$		